Titles in the History of Sports series include:

Baseball
Basketball
Football
Golf
Hockey
Skiing
Soccer
Tennis
Track and Field
Volleyball
Wrestling

TENNIS

BY VICTORIA SHERROW

LUCENT BOOKS®

THOMSON
™
GALE

San Diego • Detroit • New York • San Francisco • Cleveland • New Haven, Conn. • Waterville, Maine • London • Munich

On cover: Aletha Gibson competes at Wimbledon in 1957.

LIBRARY OF CONGRESS CATALOGING-IN-PUBLICATION DATA

Sherrow, Victoria.
    Tennis / by Victoria Sherrow.
        p. cm. — (History of sports)
Summary: A detailed history of the sport of tennis including its origins, evolution, cul-
tural and sociological aspects, major tournaments, and outstanding players.
Includes bibliographical references (p.).and index.
    ISBN 1-56006-959-7 (hardback : alk. paper)
    1. Tennis—Juvenile literature. [1. Tennis.] I, Title. II. History of sports (San Diego,
Calif.)
    GV996.5 .S53 2003
    796.342—dc21

                                                                    2001008669

Contents

More than many areas of human endeavor, sports give us the opportunity to see the possibilities in our physical selves. As participants, we all too quickly find limits to how fast we can run, how high we can jump, how far and straight we can hit a golf ball. But as spectators we can surpass those limits as we view the accomplishments of others and see how fast, how smooth, and how strong a human being can be. We marvel at the gravity-defying leaps of a Michael Jordan as he strains toward a basketball hoop or at the dribbling of a Mia Hamm as she eludes defenders on the soccer field. We shake our heads in disbelief at the talents of a young Tiger Woods hitting an approach shot to the green or the speed of a Carl Lewis as he appears to glide around an Olympic track.

These are what the sports media call "the oohs and ahhs" of sports—the stuff of highlight reels and *Sports Illustrated* covers. But to understand a sport only in the context of its most artistic modern athletes is shortsighted, for it does little justice to the accomplishments of the athletes or to the sport itself. Far more wise is to view a sport as a continuum—a constantly moving, evolving process. On this continuum are not only the superstars of today, but the people who first played the sport, who thought about rules and strategies that would make it more challenging to play as well as a delight to watch.

Lucent Books' series The History of Sports provides such a continuum. Each book explores the development of a sport from its basic roots onward, and tries to answer questions that a reader might wonder about. Who were its first players, and what sorts of rules did the sport have then? What kinds of equipment were used in the beginning and what changes have taken place over the years?

Each title in The History of Sports also identifies key individuals in the sport's history—people whose leadership or skills have made a difference in the way the sport is played today. Included will be the easily recognized names, the Mia Hamms and the Sammy Sosas, the Wilt Chamberlains and the Wilma Rudolphs. But there are also the names of past greats, people like baseball's King Kelly, soccer's Sir Stanley Matthews, and basketball's Hank Luisetti—who may be less familiar today, but were as synonymous with their sports at one time as the "oohs and ahhs" players of today.

Finally, the series looks at the aspects of a sport that are particularly important in its current point on the continuum. Baseball today is better understood knowing about salary caps and union negotiators. One cannot truly know modern soccer without knowing about the specter of fan violence at matches. And learning about the role of instant replay is critical to a thorough understanding of today's professional football games. In viewing a sport as a continuum, the strides that have been made along the way are that much more admirable. It is a richer view, and one that shows how yesterday's limits have been surpassed—and how the limits of today are the possibilities of athletes in the future.

Tennis Anyone?

Once associated with the nobility, the modern-day version of this racket sport is now a popular year-round activity for millions of people, making tennis one of the few truly global sports. As of 2001, the International Tennis Federation (ITF) estimated there were 60 million players in two hundred countries worldwide, playing on approximately 750,000 courts. About 300 million tennis balls were being sold annually. Some two hundred nations belong to the ITF, which oversees the sport and sets standards for tournament play.

Tennis is also a popular spectator sport. During the 1990s, Gallup polls showed that it ranked number four as the sport Americans most like to watch, after football, baseball, and basketball. Former champion Jimmy Connors says, "I think people play and watch tennis because it's exciting. I know that's how I feel."[1]

Through the centuries, tennis has been banned by religious leaders, blamed for the deaths of monarchs, and embroiled in political conflicts. For decades during the 1900s, people argued about whether to keep tennis an amateur sport or open tournaments to professionals, too. As tennis became more popular, the world's best players, whether amateur or professional, were allowed to enter tournaments, which offered increasingly lucrative prizes. Talented and charismatic players have drawn more fans to the game, especially after matches began appearing on television in the late 1960s.

Although tennis was once confined to manicured grass lawns at country clubs and private homes, today's game takes place both indoors and out, in many settings, and on different court surfaces. The modern player has a variety of merchandise to choose from; although tennis balls are standardized, players have many options regarding the rackets they use and the clothing they wear.

Human drama adds still more interest to the game. In singles play, one person confronts another across the net, although without physical contact. As former Davis Cup

Jimmy Connors executes a dramatic serve at the 1985 Wimbledon Tennis Championships.

captain Billy Trabert said, "There is a unique pressure on any tennis player—both weekender and tournament performer—to accept total responsibility for his performance. . . . You have no excuses."[2] Players must also make quick decisions and adjustments during each game as they strategize and run down balls. As the legendary Billie Jean King says, "You don't get a rest between plays. There are no half-times and time-outs. It's nonstop action. . . ."[3] With an array of techniques, fascinating personalities, intense rivalries, and big prizes, tennis is truly a game for all seasons.

CHAPTER 1

From "Game of the Palm" to Lawn Tennis

Unlike some games, tennis evolved over several centuries. Why exactly it is called tennis remains a mystery. The name may come from the ancient Egyptian city Tenis (Tinnis in Arabic) or from a French city called Tennis. Some historians suggest it stems from *tenez,* which can mean "take it" or "play" from the French verb *tendre*—to hold. Still others say it comes from "tens," an English word that can mean a weaver's shuttle, a device that moves back and forth, in the same way a ball moves across the court. It is also unclear how, when, or where the earliest form of this ball game was played. In any case, early versions of tennis were played in medieval Europe.

Roots in Medieval France

Since ancient times, people have enjoyed games using either their hands or a racket-like device to hit a ball. Ball games were played in present-day Latin America, Egypt, Greece, Arabia, and Rome, sometimes as part of religious rites. The Persian ball game *tchigan,* which dates back to 5 B.C., may have been the first game played with racketlike devices. The ancient Greeks also played a ball and racket game called *sphairistike.*

French troops visiting Egypt during the Crusades of the twelfth century may have seen handball games, which they brought home. Knights and Catholic monks played what the French called *jeu de paume* (game of the palm) because people used their hands to hit the ball. Players earned points by hitting the ball so their opponents could not return it. Knights used large, walled outdoor courts while monks played in open-air courtyards inside their monastery walls, using balls made from layers of cloth bound tightly into a round shape. *Jeu de paume* became so popular among monks that some church officials condemned it or even banned it, saying that it distracted monks from their religious duties.

Meanwhile, French rulers began to play, using rectangular courts divided in half with a rope or, when outdoors, a mound of earth. The outdoor game, called *long paume*, featured a longer court with up to six players per side. Boundaries were marked on the ground, and players had to hit the ball within the lines of the opposite court. In *courte-paume*, players competed on a smaller indoor court, walled around three sides to form boundaries. They could return the ball by hitting it across the net or into the wall. This game endures today as "court tennis" or "royal tennis."

Equipment changed over the years. To protect their hands, the nobility began wearing specially made leather gloves. By the 1300s, players substituted short wooden bats, followed by paddles. Balls were made entirely of cloth or with other materials: wood; wool and twine; cloth filled with hair; or leather stuffed with hair, bran, sand, or sawdust. Balls were made sturdier once people started hitting them with paddles and rackets. After strung rackets emerged in the 1500s, ball makers began producing seamed balls, which were rounder and took a livelier bounce off the racket. To avoid arguments about whether a ball actually went over the rope, people attached tassels or fringes to help stop balls that were too low. By the 1500s, full-length nets were being used to divide the court.

The object of the game remained the same—to hit the ball across the court to one's opponent in such a way that it could not be returned.

"Royal Tennis"

Jeu de paume became increasingly popular with French aristocrats, who built *jeu de paume* courts at their estates. Around 1352, the game crossed the English Channel to Scotland and England, and by 1400, courts could also be found in Italy and Germany. Outside France, the game was called "royal tennis," but the origin of the name is unclear.

The English embraced tennis, and by 1388, tennis began to replace archery as the most popular sport among the nobility. Although Henry V banned it for that reason, his ban was short-lived. Also during the late 1300s, Charles V banned Frenchmen from playing tennis, complaining that people played so often they ignored

English sportsmen enjoy a game of tennis in the 1500s.

their jobs and other responsibilities. Still, the game endured and attracted women as well as men. During the 1420s, a certain Lady Margot became known throughout France for her skill. In 1427, the fourteen-year-old accepted an invitation to play at the court of King James I, where she defeated some of Scotland's top male players.

For some monarchs, the game proved fatal. French king Louis X died in 1316 after a long match. Chilled and exhausted, the twenty-six-year-old king caught a fatal case of pneumonia. Tennis also indirectly killed King James I in February 1437. While trying to escape from assassins, he crawled into drains that led to an opening in his tennis court. Too late, he remembered the hole had been blocked because so many stray balls fell into it. James was trapped and his pursuers killed him. Tennis claimed another life in 1498 when King Charles VIII of France ran into a door while he was playing and died from head injuries.

Despite these mishaps, the sport remained popular among royalty. English king Henry VIII especially liked mixed doubles, where he played with female partners. By 1530, Henry VIII had tennis courts at four palaces: Greenwich, St. James, Hampton Court, and Whitehall, where Henry and his courtiers could use five different indoor and outdoor courts. Historians think the idea of tossing the ball into the air to serve arose because Henry was so plump he had trouble throwing the ball himself and had a servant do it for him. Tennis remained popular in England under Henry's daughter, Elizabeth I.

Likewise, the game flourished in France. During the 1500s, there were about eighteen hundred courts in Paris alone, and a court was even constructed on a French ship. In 1686 Louis XIV paid forty-five thousand francs to have an elaborate court built at his palace in Versailles.

The production of tennis equipment also flourished, and people began using strung rackets and livelier balls. By the 1700s, many balls were made from thin wool strips wound tightly around a core, then surrounded with string tied in various directions and finally covered with cloth—black for indoor play or white for playing outdoors.

England Takes the Lead

By the early 1600s, more people were playing tennis and the game had spread beyond the nobility to the middle class. In France, betting on tennis was so popular that the government outlawed public exhi-

FROM PADDLES TO RACKETS

The word "racket" may have come from the Arabic word *rahat,* meaning "palm of the hand," the medieval English word *rackle* (meaning "framework"), or the Latin word *rec* (framework). An early tennis racket was the *battoir,* which appeared in the fourteenth century and resembled a canoe paddle but with a thicker handle. During the 1400s, the Italians made wood rackets similar to those used today in paddle tennis.

The wooden center area of the racket later changed to a webbed area made of strings. By 1500, rackets were no longer made solely of wood but had strings woven inside a wooden head. The first strung rackets, made with sheep gut during the 1500s, helped the ball bounce off the racket better. Between the 1500s and 1700, rackets of different shapes and sizes were used.

Around 1750, the modern-style racket emerged: lopsided head, thick gut strings, and a longer handle. This type of racket enabled players to retrieve balls from more parts of the court and hit the ball in ways that added spins to their shots. Racket shapes included round, oval, and triangular, and sometimes resulted from particular handcrafting techniques.

Until the 1920s, the frames of modern rackets were from one piece of wood. Then manufacturers found that pieces glued together to form laminations made a more attractive and durable racket. String materials vary. Although many people think catgut, used for racket strings, comes from cats, it is actually made from sheep's intestines, frequently originating from England or Australia. Nylon is also used for racket strings.

French nobility look on (background) during an indoor tennis match in this 1750s cartoon. Tennis exhibitions were restricted in France to the wealthy during the 1700s.

bitions. As a result, tennis once again became a game for the wealthy, played on private courts. Tennis steadily declined in France in the 1700s, especially during the French Revolution when people scorned things associated with the nobility. However, more people in other European countries, including Germany, Holland, and England, embraced the game.

Beginning in the 1860s, sports became especially popular in England as the prosperous upper middle classes sought new leisure activities. Men especially liked squash rackets and court tennis, but both genders played golf, archery, and croquet, a lawn game in which people hit balls through a series of wickets.

Seeking a livelier outdoor game for both men and women, people tried new versions of tennis. In 1858, Major T.H.

Gem and J.B. Perara devised a game called *pelota* in Birmingham, England, where they marked out a court on a lawn and divided it with a net. They used a hollow rubber ball and rackets and scored *pelota* from 1 to 15 points. The name was later changed to "lawn rackets," then to "lawn tennis" in 1872 after Gem and Perara helped to form England's first lawn tennis club at Leamington Spa.

Technology aided the sport as rubber balls became available in 1845 after Charles Goodyear invented the vulcanization process. Older rubber products were unstable, freezing in cold weather and melting in the heat. Vulcanized rubber balls were bouncy but soft enough not to damage grass. In addition, early versions of the lawn mower made it easier to trim large grassy areas, making court upkeep easier.

Four ladies prepare for a game of lawn tennis in 1888.

Major Wingfield Promotes the Game

An English military officer, Major Walter Clopton Wingfield, saw commercial possibilities in tennis. During the early 1870s, he patented a kit containing balls, rackets, a net, and instructions for laying out the court. Wingfield claimed that his game, which combined features of court tennis, badminton, and squash racquets, was inspired by the ancient Greek game *sphairistike*. To individualize his game, Wingfield shaped his court like an hourglass, narrower at the net than at the baselines. He said the court should be level, but did not specify a certain surface. Grass was an obvious choice, because existing croquet courts and cricket fields could be used for Wingfield's game, officially called "the Major's Game of Lawn Tennis." In the March 7, 1874, issue of the *London Court Journal,* Wingfield wrote:

> We hear of a new and interesting game coming out, which is likely to attract

public notice, now blasé with croquet . . . it has been tested at several country houses, and has been found full of healthy excitement, besides being capable of much scientific play. The game is in a box not much larger than a double gun case, and contains, besides bats and balls, a portable court, which can be erected on any ordinary lawn and is ornamental as well as useful.[4]

That spring, ads for Wingfield's kits appeared in newspapers, military journals, and sports-oriented magazines, and people began buying them. Within months, it was more popular than croquet or badminton, attracting the Prince of Wales, members of Parliament, the Russian royal family, and customers in Canada, India, and China.

In August, Wingfield offered a new kit with slightly different rules and a modified hourglass-shaped court. He still stated that only the server could score a point. Along with equipment and instructions, Wingfield gave playing tips; for instance: "Hit your ball gently, and look well before striking, so as to place it in the corner most remote from your adversary." He said that "the proper touch" together with a "nice appreciation of strength, adds much to the delicacy and science of the game."[5]

People who lacked access to Wingfield's kits or disagreed with his approach devised their own equipment and rules. Most people favored a simple rectangle over the hourglass-shaped court. Like court shapes and sizes, net heights also varied. Sports clubs built courts, and some used Wingfield's approach while others did not. Within a few years, people abandoned his hourglass-shaped court, net height, and the scoring system of 1–15. Nonetheless, Major Wingfield had done much to promote tennis, which spread around the world.

A Great Tournament Begins

Within a few years, interest in tennis was so high that a prominent club decided to hold a tournament. The All England Croquet Club had been founded in 1868 in Wimbledon, a small town outside London, and large crowds attended its croquet tournaments until tennis took center stage. In 1876, the management added a tennis court to attract new members. The next year, it changed its name to the All England Croquet and Lawn Tennis Club.

MAJOR WALTER CLOPTON WINGFIELD

The descendant of an ancient British family, Walter Clopton Wingfield joined the British military like his father before him. After commanding a cavalry troop in China, he returned to England as a major in the early 1860s. The tall, muscular major enjoyed sports and was delighted to see how sports-minded Britain had become while he was stationed in Asia.

Noting the trend toward livelier outdoor games men and women could enjoy together, he envisioned a variation of lawn tennis. Wingfield had played many different games himself, so he was familiar with the pros and cons of badminton, squash rackets, and others. The major had also grown up hearing tennis lore. In the 1430s, Charles d'Orleans, a member of the French royal family, had been imprisoned in his family's castle in Suffolk near the Norfolk border.

Charles loved *jeu de paume* and was permitted to play it during his years at Wingfield Castle. In 1435, he also wrote what is thought to be the first poem about tennis, which Wingfield read as a child.

Moreover, despite his title and aristocratic lineage, Major Wingfield was not wealthy, so he hoped to earn money by patenting an outdoor ball-and-rackets game. Although others said his was not a true "invention," Wingfield continued to call himself the official inventor of lawn tennis. When he died in 1912, Wingfield was neither rich nor famous, and tennis had changed significantly from his original vision. However, he is remembered as the person who promoted and popularized tennis. In 1997, Walter Clopton Wingfield was inducted into the International Tennis Hall of Fame.

An early tennis tournament at Wimbledon, England, where official rules for the sport were drafted in 1882.

Since rules varied among players, the club appointed a three-man committee to draft rules for the first All England tournament. They specified a rectangular court twenty-six yards long and nine yards wide, with a net hung from five-foot-high posts on either side dropping to no less than three feet three inches at the center. Most clubs around the world adopted these rules, which became official in 1882. They remain about the same today, except that the net now hangs from posts standing three feet six inches high, with a center height of three feet.

The committee also decided to score games and matches with the four-unit system used in royal tennis, which is still employed today: point, game, set, and match. To win a game, a player must win 4 points, going from 15 to 30 to 40 to "Game," and either player can score regardless of who serves. If both players score 3 points in a game to reach a score of 40–40 (deuce), one player must then win 2 consecutive points to take the game. Players take turns serving an entire game until one player wins six games, which make up a set.

Under these rules, if each player won six games, play continued until someone won two more games. That rule has since been changed in some tournaments where tiebreakers are played. Two sets out of three win the match. In certain tourna-ments today, men must win three sets out of five. The rules for serving remain in place: Each player receives two chances per turn. A missed serve (hit outside the opponent's service box or into the net) is a "fault," and two faults (a double fault) gives the other side a point.

With the rules settled, the tennis committee posted this notice in the June 9, 1877, issue of *The Field* magazine: "The [members of the] All England Croquet and Lawn Tennis Club, Wimbledon, propose to hold a lawn tennis meeting, open to all amateurs, on Monday, July 9th, and following days. . . . Two prizes will be given—one gold champion prize to the winner, one silver to the second player."[6]

Twenty-two men entered, paying one pound each. All were sportsmen, but few had played much lawn tennis, so they used a variety of strokes and rackets. Players used relatively slow, nonaggressive strokes, and sportsmanship was considered more important than winning. Still, the most aggressive player, Spencer Gore, ultimately won the final match, held on July 19 before about two hundred spectators.

Tournament play boosted the sport, and new clubs were formed throughout England, leading to more local and regional championships. In 1888, about one hundred different clubs formed the Lawn Tennis Association (LTA). It became the official governing body for

SCORING THE GAME

The four-point scoring system used today for tennis can be traced back to the early 1400s. At first, the score was counted as 15, 30, 45, and Game, but the number 40 gradually replaced 45. Perhaps this system evolved because the number 60 was important in France during that era and a game often went to 60—four points worth 15 each. Also, medieval games often involved gambling, and some laws limited bets to sixty derniers per game. The fifteen dernier was a common French coin, so people may have bet one dernier per point during a tennis game for a total of sixty.

Certain tennis terms used today also developed during medieval times. The term "love," meaning no score, may have come from the Dutch/Flemish word *lof*, meaning "honor." Others say "love" comes from the French word *l'oeuf* (egg), which has an oval or zero shape. Furthermore, in England a duck egg means zero, as does *luff* in Scottish. The term "deuce" means players are tied and need two more points to win a game. It may have come from the French phrase *a deux du jeu*—two points away from the game—or from *a deux* (two together).

tennis in England and set international standards for the game.

Early Players Influence the Game

Tennis evolved as people honed their skills in competition. At the first Wimbledon, Spencer Gore chose to move toward the net, trying to hit the ball before it bounced—a shot sportswriters called a "volley." Some players protested the volley and asked officials to ban it. The shot remained legal, but a new rule said players must not hit the ball *before* it crossed the net. Some historians think the volley has changed tennis more than any single stroke.

Naturally, other players tried to combat the volley. At the second Wimbledon, P.F. Hadow, a Ceylon plantation owner, met Gore in the final. In his first and only Wimbledon, Hadow used a shot called the "lob" to win. When Gore came to the net, Hadow hit the ball above Gore's head so it landed deep in his backcourt.

Talented twin brothers, British players William (Willie) and Ernest (Ernie) Renshaw, added excitement during the 1880s, especially in the game of doubles in which teams of two oppose each other, which became part of tournament play. While one brother served, the other prepared to volley at the net. When opponents countered with a lob, the Renshaws retaliated with an early version of the overhead smash, hitting the ball back so forcefully it was difficult to re-

turn. Writing about the smash, player and official F.R. Burrow said, "Sheer hard smacks that sent the ball straight into the stands from its first bound were the order of the day with the Renshaws."[7]

Such tactics angered some players. After losing a match, player Herbert Lawford asked officials to ban both the lob and overhead smash, at least from doubles tennis. Lawford claimed, "They [the Renshaws] are killing the classic ground strokes."[8] However, these shots remained legal.

The Renshaws continued to dominate tennis and became celebrities. Willie won seven Wimbledon singles titles from 1881 through 1887 and in 1889, while Ernie won one in 1888. The brothers faced each other in the finals of 1882, 1883, and 1889. Tennis fans loved to watch them. During one Wimbledon, a fan who arrived after Willie's match demanded a refund, saying, "I came only to see the Renshaws. I don't want to see anyone else."[9]

Growth in Other Countries

While the British were initiating tournaments, more people in other countries began playing tennis. New clubs sprang up in Scandinavia, Spain, Germany, the Netherlands, Portugal, South America, and English colonies in India, Africa, and Asia. Courts were built in the Soviet Union (now Russia) and in Central and Eastern Europe. Fashionable resorts offered their guests tennis courts. While the

The Renshaw twins, pioneers of the overhead smash, pose in this 1880 photograph.

English preferred grass courts, the French and Italians chose clay or cement courts.

Tennis reached the United States in 1874. Dr. James Dwight of Boston may have been the first American tennis player. He promoted and played so enthusiastically that he is called the "Father of American Lawn Tennis." Others also discovered tennis that year. Mary Ewing Outerbridge of Staten Island, New York, brought a tennis set home from Bermuda, and the game was played at the Staten Island Cricket and Baseball Club that summer. The game spread to other regions, and the first official U.S. tennis club was founded in New Orleans in 1876.

In 1881, representatives from thirty-three clubs met in New York City to form the United States Lawn Tennis Association (USLTA). It standardized rules and equipment and organized tournament play, beginning with the first men's national singles championships in Newport, Rhode Island, that same year. Nineteen-year-old Richard Sears defeated twenty-four others, and he defended his title during the next five years. As more Americans took up tennis, new tournaments were launched, and tennis became a collegiate sport, primarily at elite schools.

Women's Competition

From the start, both genders played tennis, although some people thought it was inappropriate or even scandalous for women to play in public. Still, women were determined to play sports and even compete.

The first women's championships were held at the Fitzwilliam Club in Ireland, where fourteen-year-old May Langrishe captured the title in 1879. When Wimbledon held its first women's national championship in 1884, Maud Watson triumphed. Between 1882 and 1886, Watson dominated the game until hard-hitting fourteen-year-old Charlotte "Lottie" Dod beat her in 1886 at Wimbledon. Dod surprised spectators by running down every ball and hitting harder than other women. She had modeled her game after the Renshaw twins and liked to volley. In 1887, she won both the Irish and English national titles, then took her third successive Wimbledon in 1888. After taking a break from competition, Dod returned to Wimbledon in 1891 and won again for three consecutive years. During

Despite public criticism and cumbersome clothing, women remained determined to play tennis in the early 1900s.

her career, she lost only four matches and never lost at Wimbledon.

Across the Atlantic, the U.S. women's singles championships debuted at the Philadelphia Cricket Club in 1887. At age eighteen, Philadelphian Ellen Hansell became the first U.S. women's champion. Hansell later recalled the event: "Is it possible for you to envision the gallery? A loving, but openly prejudiced crowd standing within two feet of the court lines, calling out hurrahs of applause plus groans of disappointment, and some suggestive criticism, such as: 'Run to the net.' 'Place it to her left.' 'Don't dare lose this game.'"[10]

During those years, women often served with a sidearm stroke and were discouraged from playing aggressively. In her book *Tennis for Women*, Lou Eastwood Anderson urged women to value placement over power: "A woman's game does not include fancy training on volleys and fancy strokes that make huge drafts on energy, but rather emphasizes accuracy in placement."[11] Anderson claimed too much exertion might injure women and decrease their enjoyment. Despite these warnings, as well as cumbersome clothing that included hats and long dresses, women continued to become more competitive.

International Competition

International competition expanded as tennis became part of the Olympic Games in 1896 and national teams were formed. International teams began playing in 1900 after Dwight Filley Davis, a student at Harvard University, suggested the idea of Davis Cup competition and offered a large gold-lined silver punchbowl as a prize. He himself joined the first U.S. team, which played against a British team at Boston's Longwood Cricket Club. Davis Cup matches featured a growing number of national men's teams.

By 1900, over twenty-five countries had tennis clubs and tournaments and national organizations. The 1905 Wimbledon attracted seventy-one players and hundreds more fans than it had in 1877. British players dominated early tournaments, but Australians and Americans began winning, too. More Americans became familiar with tennis after President Theodore Roosevelt (1901–1909) formed his "tennis cabinet," a group of athletic U.S. officials and foreign diplomats. As the new century began, the "game of kings" had also become a game for presidents and had moved beyond castles and country homes to courts around the world.

CHAPTER 2

Country Clubs to Public Courts

During the early 1900s, lawn tennis was played mostly at country clubs, fashionable resorts, and private homes. One author portrayed an ideal setting for a tennis game: "The scene should be laid on a well-kept garden lawn. . . . Near at hand, under the cool shadow of a tree, there should be strawberries and cream, iced [wine], and a few spectators. . . . If all these conditions are present, an afternoon spent at lawn tennis is a highly Christian and beneficent pastime."[12] Most players, who learned the game through private lessons, had both money and leisure. The game was also governed by strict rules and a dress code that specified neat white attire. Entire books were written about tennis etiquette.

Most tournament players were affluent white people who had grown up with the game and could join clubs where tournaments were held. Certain groups of people, however, including Jews and African Americans, were not admitted to most country clubs, regardless of their income, and therefore had less exposure to tennis. As the years passed, however, the sport grew more diverse. Tennis began attracting players from different classes and ethnic groups, including minorities who overcame racial barriers. The sport gained more exposure and more fans from all socioeconomic groups.

Early Champions

During the early 1900s, wealthy players continued to dominate tennis championships and, since lawn tennis originated in England, the British had a head start in mastering the sport. Their national championship at Wimbledon was the foremost tournament. Certain individuals dominated Wimbledon and sometimes won it more than once.

As tennis gained international exposure, British players faced more competition. By 1914, Belgium, Germany, Italy, Hungary, Sweden, Denmark, Holland, Spain, and the United States were producing fine players. With its favorable climate and ties to England, Australia became a tennis powerhouse. In 1907, Australian

Norman Brookes became the first Wimbledon men's champion from outside Britain. Known as "the Wizard," Brookes wielded a strong serve and volley and excellent ground strokes.

Several American women also excelled during these years. Californian May Sutton became America's first international champion, winning the singles final at Wimbledon in 1905 and 1907. Despite her small frame, Sutton was muscular, hit the ball hard, and wore shorter skirts, giving her more mobility. Even after she married, May Sutton (now May Sutton Bundy) still competed. In 1930, she gave fans a

A middle-class Victorian family rests after a game of tennis. Tennis began attracting players from all social classes during the early 1900s.

dramatic moment when she broke her leg but insisted on finishing the set with a crutch. Her tennis-playing family included sisters Violet, Florence, and Ethel, and a popular slogan during their day was "It takes a Sutton to beat a Sutton."[13]

Hazel Hotchkiss, another Californian, did manage to "beat a Sutton"—both Violet and May. After marrying George Wightman in 1912, Hotchkiss played fewer tournaments while rearing her children but still garnered forty-eight U.S. singles and doubles titles, more than any other woman before 1950. In 1924, Wightman won the Wimbledon singles title and helped the first U.S. women's Olympic team win a gold medal in doubles and mixed doubles.

California continued to foster champions, including Mary K. Browne, who won the U.S. singles title in 1912, 1913, and 1914, and Helen Wills Moody, who domi-

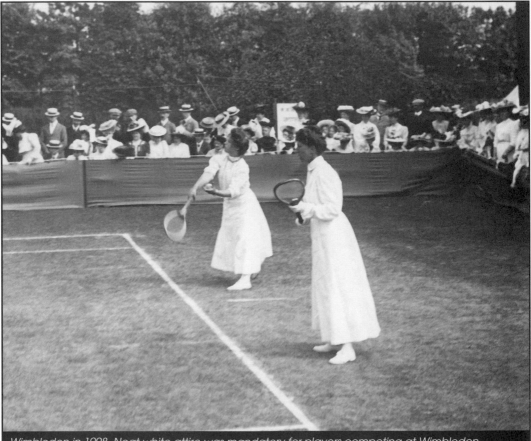

Wimbledon in 1908. Neat white attire was mandatory for players competing at Wimbledon.

American tennis legend May Sutton practices her swing in 1930 after suffering from a broken leg earlier that same year.

nated tennis during the 1920s and 1930s. Browne and Moody often played against Norwegian-American Molla Bjurstedt Mallory, who won eight Wimbledon titles: 1915–1918, 1920–1922, and 1926. Mallory captured her eighth and last U.S. women's singles title at age forty-two.

As had been true during the 1800s, the athletes' playing styles and personalities inspired fans to encourage their favorites.

New players developed strokes and playing styles that transformed tennis into a more dynamic sport—what sportswriters began calling "the big game."[14]

International Developments

As tennis became more popular, national organizations decided to form an international governing body. On March 1, 1913, twelve nations met in Paris to form the

TENNIS FASHIONS

Early tennis fashions would surprise and even amuse people today. White was the only acceptable color, and clothing was far more complicated. Men wore long trousers or knickers of wool, long-sleeved shirts, vests, neckties, and sometimes hats. In hot weather, they removed their jackets and rolled up their sleeves. In 1933, Brit Henry Wilford "Bunny" Austin, a popular player known for his sportsmanship, became the first man to walk out onto the court—in this case Wimbledon's hallowed center court—in shorts. After the initial shock wore off, other men followed, and by 1947 male players always wore shorts.

Models display the various tennis fashions of British designer Ted Tinling.

For women, long dresses with high necks were worn over corsets and layers of petticoats, along with long stockings and flat black or brown leather shoes. Hats gradually grew smaller, and women reduced the number of petticoats they wore. They also switched to white canvas shoes with rubber soles. In *A Long Way, Baby,* Grace Lichtenstein quotes Violet Sutton describing tennis wear during the early 1900s: "It was a wonder we could move at all. We wore a long undershirt, pair of drawers, two petticoats, white linen corset cover, duck shirt, shirtwaist, long white silk stockings, and a floppy hat. We were soaking wet when we finished a match."

Suzanne Lenglen revolutionized women's tennis wear in the 1920s when she doffed both petticoats and corsets. With her stylish one-piece dresses and trademark coral-colored head bandeau, Lenglen brought glamour to the women's game. Women also began wearing sailor suits, culottes (divided skirts), and even long shorts. American Gussie "Gorgeous" Moran influenced styles by raising her hemlines and wearing lacy underwear that showed when she moved.

Adding "glitz" to the sport were designers who created special tennis dresses for women stars. One of the best known was Ted Tinling, a British designer who made tennis wear for Brazil's Maria Bueno and American Billie Jean King, among others. Today players may wear various colors, although white is still required at Wimbledon. Numerous companies create stylish ready-to-wear lines for consumers, and some players endorse their own lines or a particular brand name.

International Lawn Tennis Federation (ILTF). Previously, the British Lawn Tennis Association (BLTA), which included national tennis associations from seventeen countries, had assumed the role of world governing body. The founding nations for the ILTF included Australasia, Austria, Belgium, the British Isles, Denmark, France, Germany, the Netherlands, Russia, South Africa, Sweden, and Switzerland. The United States officially joined in 1918. The ILTF began setting rules for international competition, including the Davis Cup.

World War I (1914–1918) interrupted tournament play. Afterward, Davis Cup matches resumed and became increasingly popular as tennis lovers followed their home teams. Nearly every top player participated in these national teams. During the early 1900s, English and American teams prevailed, and Americans proudly dominated Davis Cup competition for several years. Tournament results became front-page news in the United States. This made tennis more popular because, as sportswriter A. Wallis Myers wrote, Davis Cup play embodied "a rich record of international rivalry, patriotic fervor, and strenuous endeavor."[15] Players sought new ways to foil their opponents. Americans Holcombe Ward and Dwight Davis are credited with introducing the "twist service" during Davis Cup play in 1902. This serve rotates with topspin and also rotates sideways into the air, making its direction unpredictable.

In 1923, Hazel Wightman began an annual international women's team competition and offered her sterling silver "Wightman Cup" as the prize. Although Wightman envisioned a tournament for all nations, the USLTA decided that American and British teams would compete, with the winner keeping the cup that year. With Wightman as captain, the Americans won the first competition in 1924, but Britain triumphed the next year. As the Davis Cup had done for men's tennis, Wightman Cup matches heightened interest in women's tennis in both countries at a time when sports were becoming increasingly popular in America.

A Golden Age

The 1920s ushered in a golden age of sports, especially in the United States. More people became players and spectators, and sports heroes such as baseball player Babe Ruth, golfer Bobby Jones, boxer Jack Dempsey, and football player Red Grange became celebrities.

Likewise, "Big Bill" (William T.) Tilden and Suzanne Lenglen were the king and queen of tennis. More spectators came to watch these charismatic and sometimes temperamental athletes, as well as other players. Tilden helped to promote tennis in the United States, while Lenglen was the first French athlete to gain international fame. French men soon followed. In 1925, French players won both the men's and women's titles at Wimbledon, the mixed doubles, and men's doubles. The four top French male players—Jean Borotra, René Lacoste, Jacques Brugnon, and Henri Cochet—were called the "Four Musketeers" and attracted thousands of new fans.

Great rivalries fueled the increasing enthusiasm for sports. Fans wanted to see if America's "Little Bill" (William) Johnston would defeat "Big Bill" Tilden, and how either would fare against one of the "Musketeers." In a long-awaited contest, Helen Wills faced Suzanne Lenglen in 1926 in Cannes, France—their only match together. The large crowd—four thousand spectators inside the Carlton Club and another four thousand or more outside—reflected the sport's growing popularity. Wills lost that match but went on to achieve an outstanding record.

During the 1930s, Wills and America's Helen Hull Jacobs often met in the finals of tournaments. Although newspapers and magazines hinted at a "feud" between the "two Helens," sportswriter Al Laney writes, "Certainly they were rivals, as were Miss Wills and all the other girls she kept from being champion. And certainly

Helen Wills retrieves a serve in the 1935 Wimbledon semifinals.

The charismatic "Big Bill" Tilden lunges for a backhand return in 1935.

they were . . . never very friendly . . . but I am convinced there was never any active dislike."[16] Nonetheless, dramatic stories helped to sell tickets.

Years of Growth

By the 1930s, tennis players had many new tournaments to choose from, and the older tournaments were enlarged to accommodate new fans. Larger crowds had prompted the USLTA to move the men's U.S. championships to the larger and more accessible West Side Tennis Club in Forest Hills in Queens, New York, in 1915. The women's championships were also relocated there in 1921. Likewise, a spacious new grass court was laid out at Wimbledon in 1922, with a stand large enough for fifteen thousand spectators.

Players faced clay courts in France and Italy. Slow clay courts favor players with patience and strong ground strokes rather than a "serve and volley" game. In 1925, the Italian Championships were first held at Foro Italico, near Rome's Coliseum. That same year, the French Championship, which was originally limited to French citizens, was opened to amateurs of all nationalities. The famous Roland Garros Stadium was built in an elegant Paris suburb in 1928 to hold the growing number of fans. Set among picturesque trees and hills, the slow surface, made from crushed brick, also favors backcourt players who like long rallies, rather than serve-and-volley experts who do better on fast surfaces. Roland Garros has been called the most challenging surface in tennis.

In addition to large tournaments, numerous smaller tournaments were held each year. At these events, players could establish a record that would earn them invitations to enter major tournaments.

Tennis for Fun

While top players enjoyed more competitive opportunities, others took up tennis for fun. In the United States, the advent of public courts made tennis accessible to more people. During the Great Depression of the

René Lacoste, one of France's "Four Musketeers," attracts a crowd of spectators in 1925.

GRAND SLAMMERS

Just before World War II and again in 1953, two Americans made history by becoming the first players to win the "Grand Slam of Tennis," sweeping the four major international tournaments in a twelve-month period. Sportswriter Allison Danzig, who covered tennis for the *New York Times,* had coined the term in 1933. Five years later, Don Budge achieved this "first" by capturing the U.S., Wimbledon, French, and Australian titles. Tall, lanky Budge was also the first person to win the triple at Wimbledon—men's singles, men's doubles, and mixed doubles all in one year. Budge's backhand was one of his most formidable weapons. He won the U.S. and Wimbledon in both 1937 and 1938. His Davis Cup record was 25–4, and he was the only tennis player (as of 2000) to win the Sullivan Trophy, given each year to the American athlete who "by his or her performance, example and influence as an amateur, has done the most during the year to advance the cause of sportsmanship." Budge turned pro in 1939 and continued to play after World War II. He was a respected teacher and coach.

In 1953, nineteen-year-old San Diego native Maureen Connolly became the first woman to win the Grand Slam. Connolly, known as "Little Mo" because she was only five feet three inches tall, was a tough competitor who won fifty-six consecutive matches at age fourteen and lost only one match from 1951 to 1954. In 1950, she became the youngest woman ever to win the U.S. National Women's title, a feat she repeated in 1952 and 1953. In addition, Connolly earned three women's singles crowns at Wimbledon, in 1952, 1953, and 1954. By 1954, she had won nine major titles. The Associated Press named her Woman Athlete of the Year in both 1953 and 1954. A horseback riding accident that caused permanent leg damage cut short Connolly's playing career in 1954. During her brief time playing competitive tennis, she made her mark as one of its greatest players.

1930s, more courts were built on school grounds and in community playgrounds and parks. Many of them were constructed through public works programs that were organized under President Franklin D. Roosevelt's New Deal legislation. For a few dollars, people could buy a racket and balls and play tennis.

Tennis fans could also follow the sport in new ways. The first radio broadcast of a tennis game from Wimbledon came in 1937. The U.S. Championships were also broadcast on the radio, along with news of Davis Cup matches, during the early 1940s. Most Americans had radios and could follow sports events this way. Others followed the sport in newspapers and magazines, and some sportswriters began specializing in tennis.

Increased competition made tennis faster paced, as players aimed to maximize every point. Big changes were occurring with the serve. May Sutton once recalled how players served during the early 1900s, saying, "Our weakest stroke was the serve. We just hit the ball up without much windup."[17] By the 1930s, however, the serve had become a more offensive weapon. Players hit harder and added spins and slices, as well as placing the ball carefully. This added excitement for both players and fans.

Overcoming Snobbery

Some new players overcame the obstacles of class and a lack of money to become champions. The first international working-class champion was England's Fred Perry, born to a middle-class family in 1909. Although he did not belong to a country club or play tennis during his childhood, Perry's great eye-hand coordination and superb topspin forehand, which he could hit on the run, made this friendly, good-looking player a great champion. Sportswriter Al Laney says, "His game was his own, disconcerting, able to upset the other man's rhythm. This was because he could take a ball so early, could volley so well, and above all his marvelous speed on the court."[18]

In 1934, Perry won Wimbledon, becoming the first Englishman to achieve the men's singles title since 1919. Yet he felt rejected by the tennis elite. After winning the title, Perry overheard a club official congratulating his Australian opponent, Jack Crawford, and instead of receiving the customary honorary All England

Club member's necktie in person, Perry found it draped on his seat in the men's dressing room. In his 1984 autobiography, Perry recalled that "some elements in the All England Club and LTA looked down on me as a hot-headed, outspoken, tearaway rebel, not quite the class of chap they *really* wanted to see winning Wimbledon, even if he *was* English. . . . At the time, a young man with my background was bound to feel that snobbery very keenly."[19]

Perry won two more Wimbledon men's singles titles (in 1935 and 1936), as well as three U.S. titles (1933, 1934, and 1936), one French (1935), and one Australian (1935). With his partner Henry "Bunny" Austin, Perry brought the Davis Cup back to Britain after six years of French victories. In 1938, he became a pro player and also wrote newspaper columns and commentated on radio and television. Some critics said Perry traded "glory for gold" when he chose to earn money from his tennis career. Tennis was still dominated by upper-class white players who considered themselves "above" financial concerns—but that was starting to change.

New Champions Add Diversity

In the 1940s, tournament rosters became more diverse, both socioeconomically and ethnically. More minorities, including Hispanic Americans, were playing tennis

Pancho Gonzales (left) was ranked number seventeen in the U.S. in 1947.

and entering tournaments, and some became champions.

Two talented "Panchos"—Gonzales and Segura—showed that tennis was expanding past its core group of upper-class whites. Los Angeles native Richard Alonzo "Pancho" Gonzales was one of seven children in a working-class family. In 1940, at the age of twelve, Gonzalez learned to play without formal lessons after his mother bought him a fifty-one-cent racket for Christmas. Within two years, he was winning junior tournaments.

At age nineteen, Gonzales proceeded to make tennis his career and reached the finals in his first match. Although he lost, spectators were astonished when this newcomer won a set against Jack Kramer during that match. Though he lacked experience on clay and grass, Gonzales played well enough in the major East Coast tournaments to be ranked number seventeen in the United States in 1947. The next year, he became number one after winning the U.S. national title at Forest Hills, the U.S. Clay Court, and the U.S. Indoor—the first player ever to hold all three titles at once. He won the U.S. title again in 1949, in a thrilling five-set match against Ted Schroeder, the 1947 champion.

Gonzales turned professional after a few years, so he did not acquire as many Grand Slam titles (Wimbledon, U.S., French, and Australian) as some champions, but he continued to dazzle fans and opponents for decades. During the 1950s, Gonzales defeated numerous top professionals. Sportswriters praised his competitive urge, coordination, consistency, anticipation, power, and ability to execute every stroke—while making it look easy. Gene Scott writes, "He was a panther, crouched low, stalking every ball . . . searching for the kill. His moves covered sizable expanses without appearing to, while fleeter runners looked strained and tense."[20]

After retiring from competition in 1961, Gonzales returned in 1964 to defeat some newer champions, including Rod Laver and Arthur Ashe, before retiring again in his forties. Later, Gonzales competed in senior events while coaching and writing about tennis.

Pancho Segura, a native of Ecuador, became a champion despite poverty and physical problems, including a small stature and childhood rickets, a vitamin deficiency disease that causes weakening of the bones. Because his arms were weak, he hit both forehands and backhands with two hands, disguising the directions of his shots. During the 1940s, Segura's forehand was legendary, and his forehand service return was amazingly precise. Since two-handed strokes limited

his reach, he compensated with speed. Segura became a prominent instructor and coach after he stopped competing.

The versatile Maria Esther Bueno became the first Brazilian to win a major title. Known for her graceful footwork and athleticism, Bueno started playing at age nine and became national champion at fifteen. In 1958, she won her first international title, the Italian Championship, and then won three Wimbledon women's singles titles (1959, 1960, and 1964), as well as five doubles titles. Bueno also won the U.S. women's singles title in 1963, 1964, and 1966. Describing her style, one sportswriter said Bueno's "poise, artistry and exquisite touch are a joy to behold."[21]

African Americans Overcome Barriers

Because they were excluded from both the USLTA and its events, African Americans who enjoyed tennis formed their own clubs and organizations and organized their own tournaments during the early 1900s. In 1919, the American Tennis Association (ATA) became the nation's first sports organization formed by and for black Americans.

Some wealthy African Americans built private courts at their homes and helped to teach and coach promising young people, offering them the chance to compete with other talented players on their courts. One well-known tennis patron was Dr. Walter

HERO ON AND OFF THE COURT: ARTHUR ASHE

Born in Richmond, Virginia, Arthur Ashe and his brother were raised by their father, a park police officer, after their mother died in 1949 when Arthur was six. He first learned tennis from a playground coach and played on segregated public courts reserved "For Negroes Only." Soon, he was defeating older players and won several trophies before age ten. However, he was barred from some matches, including the Richmond City tournament in 1955, because of racism.

Ashe was invited to take lessons at the home of Dr. R. Walter Johnson, an affluent African American who helped numerous young athletes. At the USLTA Junior Singles Indoor Tournament in 1960, he won first place. Fans admired his grace, agility, and powerful strokes, especially his backhand. After graduating from high school in St. Louis first in his class, Ashe attended UCLA where he earned his degree and played collegiate tennis.

In 1963, Ashe won the National Clay Court title and became the first African-American to play on the U.S. Davis Cup team. He went on to win the U.S. Open (1968) and Australian Open (1970). Another triumph came in 1975 when he defeated Jimmy Connors, ten years his junior and ranked first in the world, at Wimbledon. With a wide range of shots and well-planned strategy, Ashe became the first man of color to win the men's title. For twelve years, he was among the world's top ten best male players. However, he had to retire after suffering a heart attack at age thirty-six.

Besides his titles, Ashe was known for his other contributions to athletics and humanitarian causes. He helped to found the Association of Tennis Professionals (ATP),

Arthur Ashe beat top-ranked Jimmy Connors in the 1975 Wimbledon Championships.

cochaired a group called Artists and Athletes Against Apartheid, was a spokesperson for the American Heart Association and United Negro College Fund, and developed tennis programs for inner-city youth. Ashe died in 1993 of AIDS, resulting from a blood transfusion he received during heart surgery in 1983. During his life, Ashe said he tried to follow his father's advice, as quoted in the December 21, 1992, issue of *Sports Illustrated*: "You don't get [anywhere] by making enemies. You gain by helping others."

Johnson, a physician and tennis player in Lynchburg, Virginia. Johnson helped Althea Gibson and Arthur Ashe, as well as other African American players, develop their games and make contacts that helped them enter tournaments.

Change came slowly. It wasn't until 1948 that Dr. Reginald Weir, a New York physician, became the first African American to play in a USLTA event, the U.S. Indoor Tournament.

During the 1950s, Althea Gibson became the first African American international champion. The daughter of South Carolina sharecroppers, Gibson grew up in Harlem, New York, where she played stickball and other street games. A recreational director for the Police Athletic League (PAL) saw the tall, lanky thirteen-year-old win a paddle tennis tournament and gave Gibson a used tennis racket. He showed her how to practice, and Gibson began playing at New York's Cosmopolitan Tennis Club, which accepted people of color.

In 1943, she won the ATA New York State girls' final, then won the ATA national women's title in both 1946 and 1948. By 1947, Gibson was the best African American female player in America. She won nine tournaments and hoped to compete against other top U.S. women. At the U.S. Eastern Indoor Tournament, Gibson reached the quarterfinals. She was the first black player at this event, in a year that also saw Jackie Robinson become the first African American in the modern baseball major leagues.

Gibson reached the finals of the Eastern Indoor Tournament two years later and hoped to play at Forest Hills. However, players could not play there without first proving themselves at other grass court tournaments, which were held at private clubs that banned black players. When no invitations arrived for Gibson, several prominent people took action. In a letter to the editor of *American Lawn Tennis* magazine that appeared in the July 1950 issue, former U.S. champion Alice Marble decried bigotry in tennis. She urged the USLTA to give Gibson the opportunity to enter top tournaments.

As a result, Gibson was invited to the Eastern Grass Courts Championships in Orange, New York. Later that year, she became the first African American to play at Forest Hills. She won her first match in two sets but lost in the second round. Although Gibson did not win any major titles for a few years, she was ranked number seven in the world in 1953 and number twelve in 1954. That year, she won the French, Italian, Asian, and Indian national titles and reached the finals at the U.S. Championships.

By 1957, Gibson had captured several major titles. Despite high temperatures and stiff competition at Wimbledon, she won every set on her way to becoming the

Althea Gibson, the first African American international tennis champion, in play during the 1956 women's quarterfinals at Wimbledon.

first black champion. Describing her victory, a London journalist wrote, "[It] shows that somewhere in the great American dream there is a place for black as well as white."[22]

Gibson then won the National Clay Court Championship and the 1957 U.S. women's title, and successfully defended her Wimbledon and U.S. titles in 1958.

Ranked number one in both 1957 and 1958, she retired from amateur tennis in 1959 to play exhibition tennis. Later, she became a pro golfer and the first black member of the Ladies' Professional Golf Association.

Gibson opened doors for minorities. As the 1960s began, diversity continued to change the game as new champions emerged from the middle and lower classes. The first African American male international champion, Arthur Ashe, grew up playing on public courts and was the first great black player to emerge from a public-parks instruction program. To make tennis more accessible to young people who lacked opportunities to play, Ashe joined with players Charlie Pasarell, Gene Scott, and Sheridan Snyder to found the National Junior Tennis League in 1969. The league, which is still active, has promoted tennis instruction in schools and recreation centers.

In 1959, Pancho Gonzales described the huge evolution in tennis, saying,

> Once the game belonged to the white flannel, polo-coated set. Not only did a player have to learn the book of social etiquette backwards, and grip a racket properly, he had to be able to lift a cup of tea without spilling a drop. . . . There were no so-called "wrong side of the tracks players." . . . [Then] tennis became the people's game. Public courts mushroomed. Expensive clothes for players were unnecessary. All a man needed was a drugstore T-shirt, a pair of cheap shorts, dime-store socks. . . . Audiences became more plebeian, more demonstrative. Where formerly ripples of applause rewarded shotmakers, there were now roars of appreciation from the shirtsleeved masses and even choruses of boos directed at bad calls.[23]

By the 1950s, tennis players were definitely more diverse. Some players were professionals, although few pros earned significant incomes. A new era would enable players to support themselves playing tennis, and their personalities and competitiveness would change the game in extraordinary ways.

CHAPTER 3

A Booming Professional Era

By 1960, tennis players had more competitive opportunities than ever before. Although major championships were played on different court surfaces and in different settings, they shared one important feature: Only amateurs could compete. Since the 1870s, the notion of playing tennis for money was considered wrong, even vulgar.

During the early 1900s, players who became professionals usually became teachers or coaches. As professionals who earned their income from tennis, they could no longer compete in the U.S., French, Australian, Wimbledon, or other top tournaments, because tennis governing organizations banned members from playing, teaching, coaching, writing about tennis, or appearing in films for pay. Play-

ers must be members in good standing of these organizations to compete.

These rules met the needs of the upper class, but deterred athletes who needed to earn a living. Unlike the rich, they could not spend their twenties and thirties living on the limited expense allowances permitted by the ILTF and other organizations that governed amateur tennis. As tennis became less elite, more players sought professional opportunities beyond teaching or coaching. Both players and fans pushed officials to open tournaments to pros.

Early Pro Matches

As early as the 1920s, some well-known players were joining pro tours. These matches usually featured players who had won at Wimbledon or the U.S. Open. The first series of pro tennis matches began on October 9, 1926, at Madison Square Garden in New York City. Businessman Charles C. Pyle had agreed to pay Suzanne Lenglen about one hundred thousand dollars to play against American Mary K. Browne, who had been ranked sixth in the world in 1925; American Vincent Richards and French Paul Feret competed as the male duo. Throughout the year, Pyle's events, held in different cities, were profitable.

Officials criticized this development. Writing for *American Lawn Tennis* magazine, one observer said, "As to the future of professional tennis, it does seem that the outlook is dark. Unless the competitive element can be introduced into the professional game—by open tournaments or in some other way—the idea is sure to fail."[24]

Pyle's tour dissolved the next year. Players tried to organize their own events, but with little success. The USLTA considered sponsoring an open tournament for amateurs and professionals in 1930, but lacked support from the ILTF. Although England approved, every other member opposed it. Despite more support for open events, the ILTF actually tightened its rules and limited amateurs to eight tournaments a year.

In 1934, a new pro tour commenced when Bill Tilden, Ellsworth Vines, Vincent Richards, and Bruce Barnes played at Madison Square Garden. Although sixteen thousand people attended the first events, interest waned because there were not enough new top pros to offer stiff competition. In 1936, a new pro event at Madison Square Garden failed.

Nonetheless, another match was held there in January 1937. Fred Perry and Ellsworth Vines played before eighteen thousand people, the largest audience in pro matches to that date. In 1938, Perry and Vines played more than fifty matches, and in 1939, Vines toured with Grand Slam winner Don Budge.

"Shamateurism"

In 1933, the USLTA and ILTF again discussed open tournaments, but still lacked enough support to change the rules. In 1934, however, the ILTF did rule to let players collect reasonable reimbursement for daily expenses while competing. The allowance was small—about twenty-eight dollars per day plus airfare in 1967.

People sidestepped the rules, however. Players could collect money for two sets of airplane tickets when they played in two nearby tournaments, though they paid for only one trip. Tennis patrons also supplied players with food, lodging, and gifts. The line between pro and amateur became increasingly blurred as players received money under different pretexts. To sell tickets, tournament sponsors offered top players appearance fees disguised as "expense" money or "hospitality allowances." Sportswriter Harry Gordon described some creative ways players received cash:

> Sometimes they would perform some simple feat like jumping over a suitcase on a 'bet'; sometimes they would be asked to play poker, knowing that their hand was loaded with aces; sometimes they might just find an envelope packed with bills wedged inside one of their shoes in the locker room. . . . Continental officials used to bet Suzanne Lenglen's father 1,000 pounds (sterling) that she wouldn't arrive for a certain tournament. She would turn up and he would pocket the 1,000 pounds.[25]

This practice was called "shamateurism." Critics called it a "sham" that players could collect large sums of money while calling themselves "amateurs." Pancho Gonzales described the hypocrisy: "In tennis the difference between an amateur and a professional player is related to the phantom table. The amateur receives money under it, the professional over it. Today, a sought-after amateur can make from $8,000 to $10,000 yearly; yet in the eyes of the public he is pure as a virgin snow drift."[26]

A Heated Debate

During World War II, the USLTA temporarily allowed amateurs to play in exhibition matches benefiting the Red Cross and other wartime charities. After the war ended in 1945, however, the old rules banning professionals from tournaments were reinstated.

More players wanted to earn money at their sport, so the pro tours expanded. Two Americans, Bobby Riggs and Don Budge, faced each other in 1947. That same year, Bill Tilden organized his Professional Players Association, featuring himself and Fred Perry. Their group became part of the World Professional Tennis League (WPTL), which also featured women. Pauline Betz and Gertrude "Gussie" Moran, a glamorous player known for her lace-trimmed panties, competed against each other.

The pro tour expanded further after WPTL organizer Jack Harris signed Jack Kramer, Bobby Riggs, Pancho Segura, and Dinny Pails. Kramer, who won the U.S. Men's Championship in 1946 and 1947 and Wimbledon in 1947, became executive director of the Association of Tennis Professionals (ATP). He helped to organize the pros and negotiated better contracts for them. ATP athletes played numerous matches throughout the United States.

In 1948, ATP players Riggs, Segura, Kramer, Gonzales, Frank Kovacs, and Welby Van Horn became the first pros to tour Australia, playing matches sponsored by the *Philadelphia Enquirer.* Tennis was something of a national sport in Australia, and large crowds attended these matches. In

1952, Frank Sedgman and Ken McGregor became the first Australian pro tennis players. In 1953, they played against Kramer and Segura, respectively. The next tour featured exciting matches between Sedgman and Gonzales and Segura and Budge.

In 1957, the USLTA again seriously discussed opening tennis to professionals. E. C. Potter writes, "Other nations, too, were changing their views. . . . It had been a long time since all tennis players had been true amateurs."[27] Three years later, the ILTF considered opening some tournaments to pros. But when members voted on this measure in 1962, it failed to pass, despite support from Britain, the United States, France, and Australia.

During these years, more top players turned professional. Without them, Wimbledon and other tournaments featured less competition, and ticket sales dwindled. "Shamateurism" aroused increasing criticism, and players complained that the national and international tennis organiza-

American Bobby Riggs was one of six ATP pros to tour Australia for the first time in 1948.

THE TIEBREAKER

In 1965, Jimmie Van Alen introduced the sudden death tiebreaker in Newport, Rhode Island. Players who were tied at six games all had to play a nine-point sudden death tiebreaker, and the first player to reach five points won the set. This method was used at the U.S. Open from 1970 to 1974. People had differing opinions about the sudden death tiebreaker, which was more exciting for spectators than for the players. Some of the top players of the day—Arthur Ashe, John Newcombe, and Pancho Gonzalez for example—disliked it, saying that luck played too big a role. In his book *My Life with the Pros,* Bud Collins recalls that Arthur Ashe said, "It's eerie what the tiebreakers do. Those flags are out and the crowd is absolutely silent." Cliff Drysdale called them "extraordinarily nerve-wracking."

Critics suggested that a tiebreaker should require a person to win by at least two points and with more than just five points. The twelve-point tiebreaker, called the "lingering death" tiebreaker, was introduced in 1975 and is now used in major tournaments throughout the world. Each player or doubles team must win seven points to take the tiebreaker and set—but by a margin of two points. So the winner might take the tiebreaker with a score of 7–5, 8–6, 9–7, and so on.

tions wielded too much control over players and competitions.

By the late 1960s, tennis associations had been debating "open tennis" for decades. Finally, it happened.

The "Open Era" Begins

In 1968, Wimbledon officials made a dramatic and long-awaited announcement: Both amateurs and professionals were invited to compete at the All England championships. Critics of shamateurism applauded this news and looked forward to events featuring all the best players. Tennis writer Al Laney says their decision was made "for the good of the game" and that "Wimbledon sought to make its tournament in fact, as well as name, the world's premier tennis event, and to have

the title of world champion it would bestow on the winner, mean exactly that."[28]

The ILTF then met to reconsider open tennis. Eighty-six representatives from forty-seven of the sixty-five ILTF member nations attended the historic meeting where they unanimously approved the measure. Bob Kelleher, then president of the USLTA, said, "It was an incredible result achieved here in a spirit of highest cooperation and friendliness."[29]

The status quo did not change overnight. At first, the ILTF succumbed to pressure from Eastern European countries and established four different classifications of players. Tennis historian Bud Collins describes them:

1. Amateurs, who would not accept prize money.

2. Teaching professionals, who could compete with amateurs only in open events.

3. "Contract professionals," who made their living playing tennis but did not accept the authority of their national associations affiliated to the ITF, signing guaranteed contracts instead with independent promoters.

4. "Registered players," who could accept prize money in open tournaments but still accepted the authority of their national associations and retained eligibility for amateur events including the Davis, Federation and Wightman Cups.[30]

Within a few years, however, these distinctions disappeared and players no longer had to consider their status as "amateur" or "professional."

The ILTF sanctioned twelve open events in 1968, beginning with the British Hard Court Championships, held in Bournemouth, England, in April. Top players who were already competing in World Championship Tennis (WCT) could not attend, and several top amateurs also did not enter. Four top women (also the only women pros at that time)—Billie Jean King, Rosemary (Rosie) Casals, Ann Haydon Jones, and Francoise Durr—were also committed to play elsewhere. However, several top men competed, and Australia's Ken Rosewall won the top prize of one thousand pounds.

Rod Laver triumphed at Wimbledon in 1962, earning $4,800.

England's Virginia Wade won the women's title (and three hundred pounds) for the second consecutive year.

The world's finest players competed that June at Wimbledon, where Rod Laver, who had won in 1962, triumphed again and received $4,800 (U.S.). At the U.S. Open that fall, players vied for $100,000 in prizes—the largest total thus far.

Spectators enjoyed the intense competition. Sportswriter Linda Timms, who saw this match, wrote that "there is nothing bizarre or shocking about amateurs

"BATTLE OF THE SEXES"

On September 20, 1973, Billie Jean King faced Bobby Riggs in a major media event called the "Battle of the Sexes." The fifty-five-year-old Riggs had won the triple at Wimbledon, then turned pro in 1948. By the 1970s, he was known more for his flashy personality and as a "hustler" who bet on tennis events. Riggs claimed that any male pro could beat a top woman player, and he decided to prove it by defeating Margaret Smith Court in a match in 1973.

King then challenged Riggs to a best-of-five-set match. Promoters decided to stage their showdown at the Houston Super-dome with a prize of one hundred thousand dollars—winner take all. The event was heavily publicized, and both players gave interviews. According to George Gipe in *The Great American Sports Book,* before the match, Riggs told one reporter, "She's a great player for a gal. But no woman can beat a male player who knows what he's doing. I'm not only interested in glory for my sex, but I also want to set women's lib back . . . to send women back into the home where they belong."

The match became far more than a sports event and polarized Americans along gender lines. People who supported feminism rooted for King, while those who opposed it supported Riggs. More than thirty thousand spectators bought tickets, and an estimated 40 million people in thirty-six countries watched the match on television. As the match proceeded, each player won four games before King took the first set 6–4. Riggs, who looked tired, lost the next two sets 6–3, 6–3.

The match was considered a major breakthrough for women and became part of sports history. Describing the event in the *Cincinnati Post* in 1998, journalist Janet Graham said, "A quarter of a century later, the idea that a tennis match could force social change almost seems preposterous. But for those who witnessed King's victory, it was the first glimpse at a new era for women in sports and in life."

Billy Jean King (top) battles Bobby Riggs in the 1973 "Battle of the Sexes."

Stan Smith in action. Smith was ranked number one among U.S. men in 1969.

playing professionals. On the contrary, it seemed natural, straightforward and obvious, and one could only wonder why it had never happened before."[31]

Other sportswriters agreed that open tennis eliminated the hypocrisy of shamateurism. Lance Tingay wrote, "There is now no need for the lawn tennis enthusiast to gaze bleakly at his friends, to shift uneasily from one foot to another and try to explain that that word 'amateur' is a technical definition that has nothing to do with not making money from the game. He can tell his friends, in fact, that the amateur and professional distinction is really dead."[32]

Great Players Fuel the "Boom"

As open tennis created more competition, players had to stay sharp to gain prizes and top rankings. Young people watching these dynamic matches realized they could make a living playing tennis, and more of them pursued the sport.

Interest also grew in the players themselves, as talented veterans and newcomers produced thrilling matches. In 1969, forty-one-year-old Pancho Gonzales managed to defeat several younger champions to win the fifty thousand dollar Howard Hughes Open in Las Vegas and the Pacific Southwest Open title. That same year, American Stan Smith, age twenty-three, became number one among U.S. men after winning eight tournaments. For eleven years, Smith also boosted the U.S. Davis Cup team.

Australian players, such as Lew Hoad, Ken Rosewall, Roy Emerson, Fred Stolle, Mel Anderson, John Newcombe, and Rod Laver, delighted fans with their talent and good humor. Known for his forceful serve, volley, and forehand, Newcombe won Wimbledon and the U.S. Open in 1967 and two more Wimbledons (1970, 1971). At age thirty-three, Rosewall won a second French title in 1968, was U.S. champion in 1970, and gained two more Australian titles (1971, 1972). He defeated Laver at the WCT championship in 1971 and again in 1972 in what sportswriters call one of history's best matches. Between 1960 and 1975, Australian Margaret Smith Court won a record-setting sixty-two titles in singles, doubles, and mixed doubles.

By the late 1970s, more players from various countries reached the top. Sweden's Bjorn Borg, Argentina's Guillermo Vilas, and Romania's Ilie Nastase played in numerous finals, while Czechoslovakia's Martina Navratilova and Holland's Betty Stove ignited women's tennis.

Great rivalries added more excitement. During the early seventies, Billie Jean King and Chris Evert played memorable matches as Evert moved into the top spot King had held for several years. Evert versus Evonne Goolagong was another big

John Newcombe stood out among other Australian pros with his powerful serve and forceful swing.

Czech-born Martina Navratilova's offensive strategy of tough serves and strong volleys led her to victory at Wimbledon in 1978.

draw. Although Evert defeated Goolagong 21–12 overall, Goolagong won four of the five major tournaments where they faced each other in the finals during the 1970s.

From 1975 to 1982, the number one ranking went back and forth between Evert and Martina Navratilova. Navratilova dominated from 1982 to 1987, but Evert continued to challenge her until she retired in 1990. Fans enjoyed watching their different styles: Evert showed little emotion and

played more at the baseline, while the more volatile Navratilova tried to score on serves and volleys. When Navratilova finally won Wimbledon in 1978, fans were touched when Evert hugged her rival.

Among the men, the famous rivalry between Jimmy Connors and Bjorn Borg thrilled fans. Their 1976 U.S. Open final is considered one of the best matches in history. During four long sets, each won dramatic points, often returning the ball numerous times. Borg faced another tough opponent, John McEnroe, in the final rounds of major tournaments.

During the 1990s, men's finals often featured Pete Sampras, Stefan Edberg, Patrick Rafter, and Andre Agassi, while women's final rounds included Steffi Graf, Monica Seles, Arantxa Sanchez Vicario, Gabriela Sabatini, Hana Novotna, Lindsay Davenport, Jennifer Capriati, and Martina Hingis.

Record Breakers

These players also gave fans some historic moments. In 1979, Billie Jean King broke a major record by winning her twentieth Wimbledon title (combining singles and doubles), after she and Martina Navratilova won the doubles crown. King's record, which exceeded Elizabeth Ryan's nineteen titles, included six singles, ten doubles, and four mixed doubles from 1961 to 1979.

Jimmy Connors, star of the 1976 U.S. Open.

In 1982, crowd pleaser Jimmy Connors excited fans with a surprising "comeback." At age thirty, he defeated John McEnroe at Wimbledon and Ivan Lendl at the U.S. Open. In 1991, Connors, then thirty-nine, became the second-oldest semifinalist in U.S. Open history. Fans screamed as "the old man" entered the

WORLD TEAM TENNIS

World Team Tennis (WTT) was launched in 1973 with lawyer-businessman Larry King as founder and president. Match play began the next year, and sixteen American cities initially sponsored teams. After five seasons, WTT folded and was reorganized as TeamTennis. Players competed in both singles and doubles matches. Unlike USLTA events, fans were encouraged to be loud and expressive during the matches. TeamTennis matches were scheduled for five weeks each year from late June to early September. Players on the various teams have included Billie Jean King, Jimmy Connors, Chris Evert, Martina Navratilova, and Tracy Austin. The teams included both men and women, and matches were held in cities around the country. Among the top teams were the Philadelphia Freedoms and New York Apples, which won the WTT title in both 1976 and 1977. They were coached by King, the first woman player ever to coach men when she led this team. Before being traded to the Apples, King had been a player-coach for the Philadelphia Freedoms.

court. Pleased, Connors said, "It was 20,000 people making the sound of 60,000."[33] The next year, in a new "Battle of the Sexes" match in Las Vegas, Connors defeated Martina Navratilova in two sets. Meanwhile, Navratilova also made history by winning the Grand Slam in doubles events twice in the 1990s.

In 1988, Steffi Graf became the first person to win a Golden Grand Slam and just the third woman in history to win the Grand Slam. As of 2001, Graf remained the only player to win a Grand Slam on four different surfaces: carpet, clay, grass, and hard court.

The 1990s saw more records broken. At the 1996 French Open, Steffi Graf won her nineteenth Grand Slam singles title. Previously, Helen Wills Moody had won nineteen Grand Slam titles, while Margaret Court had won twenty-four. In 1999, Graf surpassed Moody with twenty-two titles. Then, in 2000, Pete Sampras won his seventh Wimbledon to hold thirteen Grand Slam titles, surpassing Roy Emerson's record of twelve. Sally Jenkins wrote, "Sampras is . . . reaching for a piece of history and doing so with the kind of physical grace and talent that comes along once in a generation, found only in the Lavers, Michael Jordans, Joe Montanas, and Wayne Gretzkys."[34]

Growth in Women's Tennis

Starting in the 1970s, female players enjoyed more events, increased prize money,

Steffi Graf struggles for the return during a match at the U.S Open.

and more publicity. Some became "superstars," as female athletes became role models in an era that prized physical fitness for both genders.

Women's tennis soared after all-women tours and coed team tennis debuted in that decade. Billie Jean King, Virginia Wade, and Margaret Smith Court dominated the early open era, but new players soon challenged them. In 1971, sixteen-year-old Chris Evert captivated fans at her first U.S. Open. Her hair ribbons, earrings, and stylish dresses gave the sport a more "feminine" image as she belted out powerful ground strokes.

Women pros criticized the disparity in prize money for male and female players. Men sometimes received ten times more than women, and top-ranked women often did not earn enough to cover tournament-related expenses. Gladys Heldman, a former player turned Houston businesswoman, strongly advocated equal prize money. After founding *World Tennis* magazine in 1953, she used it as a forum to advance the sport, especially women's tennis. She suggested that women form their own tours to gain more prize money and recognition.

In 1970 Heldman and Billie Jean King did just that. King and some other players announced that unless prizes were increased, they would boycott a tournament in Los Angeles to play instead in Houston at a new $7,500 event sponsored by Virginia Slims cigarettes. Their efforts were successful, and the Virginia Slims tour was launched the next year with a total of $309,000 in prizes. King won $117,000 on the 1971 Slims tour, becoming the first woman athlete to earn $100,000 in one year. Between 1970 and 1972, women's prize money rose from about $50,000 to $1 million annually, and it has continued to rise.

The feminist movement also boosted women's tennis as women sought equal opportunities in employment, education, and other areas of life. In 1972, a federal law called Title IX was passed as part of the Educational Amendments Act mandating equal opportunities in educational programs, including athletics. It reads, in part: "No person in the United States shall, on the basis of sex, be excluded from participation in, be denied the benefits of, or be subjected to discrimination under any educational program or activity receiving federal financial assistance."[35] Schools had to follow this law or risk losing federal funding. Before Title IX, schools and colleges often devoted most of their athletic budgets, as much as 99 percent, to men's sports. After 1972, they increased budgets for women's sports programs, including tennis.

Chris Evert, seen here, dazzled onlookers with her powerful strokes and stylish attire.

Billie Jean King advocated prize equity for women athletes.

while women's matches were the best of three. However, others noted that women's tennis was just as important to fans and even offered special attractions, such as longer point play. Male players tend to end points faster with a service ace or a rush to the net. Although women also could serve and volley well, frequently they hit more shots, so recreational players could relate to their game better.

Billie Jean King became a fiery advocate for women's tennis. In 1974, she and her husband, Larry King, founded a new magazine called *WomenSports,* which served as another forum for King's views and a means to promote women's athletics in general. Coverage of tennis in the print media and television drew more fans and players to the game.

Growth of Recreational Tennis

During the 1970s, tennis became a favorite sport for middle-class Americans as well as people in other countries. Nielsen surveys showed that the number of Americans who played tennis rose from about 10.3 million in 1970 to 20.2 million in 1973. By 1976, 33.9 million Americans said that they played the game "from time to time"; more than half played at least a few times each month.[36] Between 1970 and 1982, the number of women playing recreational tennis rose from about 3 million to 11 million.

Still, most women players earned less than men, and they pushed for total equity in prize money at national and international tournaments. In 1973, prizes for male and female champions did become equal at the U.S. Open, but many other tournaments did not follow suit. Opponents to prize equity contended that the differences were justified, because men playing at Wimbledon and certain other events had to win three out of five sets,

Recreational tennis clubs like this one became increasingly popular in the 1970s and the 1980s.

The number of spectators also rose, as shown by a Harris poll taken in 1974. Pollsters announced, "The number [of fans] who say they 'follow' tennis has risen from 17 to 26 percent just in the last year, by far the most dramatic change in American sports preferences."[37]

Thousands of new tennis courts and facilities were built around the United States, including more indoor courts, sometimes air-conditioned, for year-round play. New kinds of indoor and outdoor court surfaces were easier to maintain.

During these boom years, tennis clubs became big business, and professionals found jobs as instructors and club managers. People of all ages took lessons and competed in amateur singles and doubles events in their clubs and communities. Tennis clubs became a popular place to socialize, as well as to play and watch matches.

New Equipment and Techniques

Sales of tennis gear surged, too, during the boom. Manufacturers provided new kinds of balls and rackets, as well as fashionable tennis clothing and accessories. New styles and colors replaced the conservative clothing of earlier decades, and looked better on color television, although Wimbledon continued to require traditional whites. The new attire appealed to consumers, who bought these stylish new sports clothes for recreational play.

Technology strongly influenced the game. Modern pressurized tennis balls were engineered to be bouncier than earlier versions. By the 1970s, balls were made with a core formed from two halves of rubber and outer covers of wool, nylon, and dacron, with eighteen pounds of pressure injected inside. The color changed from white to electric yellow, which was more visible on television. Yellow balls debuted at Wimbledon in 1986.

Rackets changed greatly in terms of size, materials, and even shape. Throughout most of the 1900s, rackets had remained much the same, made from different kinds of wood, which was laminated to prevent warping or problems caused by humidity and changing temperatures. When not in use, rackets were kept in presses—frames that were screwed on to hold the racket flat—to retain their shape.

During the 1960s, racket makers tried using metal, which was lighter than wood. While wooden rackets weighed between twelve and fourteen ounces, new versions weighed ten ounces or less, with open throats that reduced air resistance and aided mobility. Billie Jean King first used

Wilson's metal racket at the 1967 U.S. Open, and Jimmy Connors popularized Wilson's T-2000. Steel and aluminum became popular materials, followed by plastic, fiberglass, graphite, and various combinations. By the 1980s, graphite and composites had become the most popular racket materials.

Racket sizes also changed. In 1976, the Head company introduced the "Prince Classic," which had an enlarged hitting space. Despite initial resistance, people gradually accepted the Prince and began to prefer larger rackets, which eventually came in four sizes: standard, midsize, oversize, and super oversize.

Bouncier balls and new kinds of rackets made tennis even more dynamic. Players had to refine their entire game, including stamina and mental toughness, to win. More and more, especially in men's tennis, players aimed to win points immediately with a big serve, called an "ace" when the opponent can't return it or touch it. Modern hard court surfaces further enhanced a fast serve. And though some male players of the 1970s produced serves clocked at ninety miles per hour, the next decade would see even speedier serves and a faster game than ever.

CHAPTER 4

A Popular Commercial Sport

By the late 1900s, tennis was both a big business and a popular form of entertainment. The last decades of the twentieth century brought some of the best matches in history, as well as new records and "firsts" in the sport. "Tennis fever" reached all-time highs, with more tournaments and fans than ever before. The number of spectators rose as more people attended tennis events and more people watched televised matches. The media, which included new cable networks, some devoted exclusively to sports, began to cover many team and individual events. Television watchers could enjoy tennis matches, either contemporary or taped matches from the past, on any day of the week. Spectators enjoyed top-

notch competition, as talented individuals from various countries vied for high rankings and added their personal flair to the game.

Also popular were pro-celebrity tournaments where actors and other celebrities played doubles matches with professional tennis players. These star-studded events, which were often held on the West Coast of the United States, where many celebrities live, or in other chic European locations like Monaco, raised money for charities. Some were broadcast on television. Tennis was also the subject of several feature films, such as *Players*, and top-rated television shows, including *Charlie's Angels* and *Macmillan and Wife,* aired episodes with tennis plots. Continuing exposure kept tennis in the public eye and reinforced its status as a fun and trendy sport.

Tennis now had become a blend of old traditions and modern innovations and equipment. The court layout and basic rules and tools—a ball and racket—remained much the same for over a century, but equipment and techniques changed. Strokes were hit with much more power, and court surfaces included grass, clay, cement, carpet, and composition. Furthermore, players with talent and "star quality" could make a great deal of money.

Sponsors Boost Tournament Opportunities

Rising interest in tennis drew more commercial sponsors, which, in turn, increased prize money. Growing tournament budgets attracted still more players to become professionals.

Some sponsors supported the same tournaments each year, while others backed individual events. One large new tournament series was the Grand Prix, which debuted in 1970 and was sponsored by Pepsico. That year, there were nineteen Grand Prix tournaments for men. In 1971, the Grand Prix expanded to include $1.5 million in prizes. Through the years, different corporations, including Colgate-Palmolive, sponsored the Grand Prix until it was disbanded in 1989.

During the 1970s, more sponsors joined the tennis bandwagon, which especially helped to boost women's tennis. The Women's International Tennis Association, now the Women's Tennis Association

Spectators fill the stands at Wimbledon.

(WTA), established the Virginia Slims Championship in 1972, and it became a premier women's event, featuring the top sixteen players. After Virginia Slims ended its sponsorship in 1978, Avon, a huge cosmetics and jewelry firm, agreed to fund the "Avon Futures" tournaments, which replaced the Virginia Slims tour. In 1994, the event became known simply as the WTA Tour Championship. Since 1979, WTA matches have been played at New York City's Madison Square Garden.

WOMEN'S FEDERATION CUP

Women's international team tennis also expanded during the late 1900s. The Federation Cup had replaced Wightman Cup competition in 1963 as the international team competition for women. Wightman Cup matches became too predictable, as the U.S. team usually won. Federation Cup play included teams from around the world, and prize money became available in 1976. Women play Federation Cup matches for one week in one location, whereas Davis Cup matches last nine or ten weeks and are held in more than one city. Teams of four women play two singles matches and two doubles matches, and while two different women must compete in the singles matches, any combination may play the doubles. Between 1963 and 2000, the U.S. team gained the most victories—seventeen—followed by Australia with seven. Participation has grown from 36 teams in 1988 to 103 in 2000.

Tournament sponsors have included companies specializing in athletic equipment but also insurance companies, electronics companies, automobile manufacturers, telecom companies, publishers, and food and beverage companies. Players could pick and choose from numerous events around the world and compete every week of the year if they wished. Some top players even skipped the Australian Open and other Grand Slam tournaments to play in more lucrative events.

Since players had many choices, some tournaments saw dwindling rosters and ticket sales. For example, during the 1970s, some top players skipped the Australian Open more than once, because this tournament was held around the Christmas season, which some players considered inconvenient. The facility at Kooyong in Melbourne was also outdated and crowded, and its grass courts were in poor condition. As players opted to play in other tournaments, the Australian Open suffered from a lack of top names and talent. In 1980, tournament officials took action. At a cost of more than $100 million, financed by the government, they planned a new National Tennis Center at Flinders Park in Melbourne. The facility, which included an open-close roof, seated fifteen thousand people. When the Australian Open debuted at this state-of-the-art tennis center in 1988, it drew more players and fans, and intense television coverage over a two-week period attracted major commercial sponsors. A tennis-loving nation had made a large investment in the sport, and it paid off.

Big Earning Opportunities

By the 1990s, tennis prizes were richer than ever. Players also received free clothing, equipment, and other gifts, such as automobiles, from companies that wanted to associate their brand names with certain players.

The U.S. Open was a prime example of the increased prize money. In 1992, the total prize money reached $8,556,600. Beginning in 1973, prizes for the men's and women's champions became equal, and in 1992 each winner received $500,000. Prizes at Wimbledon also rose. In 1997, the total amount was increased by 6.5 percent to $11.223 million (U.S.). The men's champion received $676,450, and the women's champion received $608,805.

Tournaments also yielded large profits for their sponsors, who sold tickets, refreshments, and a variety of tennis-related items during events. For example, in 1990 the surplus at the Wimbledon Championships, sponsored by the All England Club, was 10 million British pounds. Although center court does not display advertisements, the All England Club has endorsed various tennis and nontennis products. It franchised a Flying W trademark in 1978 and has earned about $50 million annually with this logo.

The ATP tour also expanded and became more lucrative. In 1990, the tour featured seventy-five tournaments on six continents. The Grand Slam Cup, run by the ITF, culminated in a $6 million event in Munich, Germany. Winner Pete Sampras took home $2 million from this single tournament.

Women have enjoyed new opportunities on the Sanex WTA tour, which became a leading women's tour at the turn of the twenty first century. In 2002, more than one thousand players from a total of seventy-six nations were scheduled to compete for more than $51 million in prizes at sixty-six events in thirty-three countries.

Commercial Endorsements

Top tennis players can earn even more through commercial endorsements than they do playing in tournaments. Professional agents negotiate lucrative fees for endorsements for the players they represent. Top players may sign with large management firms, such as ProServe or IMG (International Management Group). Although players once endorsed only shoes, rackets, balls, and sports clothing, by the 1980s they were endorsing a vast array of products, many of them unrelated to athletics—food products, beverages, cosmetics, jewelry, automobiles, pharmaceuticals, and other things. During the 1990s, Pete Sampras appeared in an ad for the dairy industry, while Monica Seles promoted "No Excuses" Jeans. The ever-popular Jimmy Connors and Chris Evert, who had been engaged briefly during the 1970s, did a humorous commercial for an over-the-counter painkiller. In 2001, John McEnroe was featured in ads for long-distance telephone service. Both Chris Evert and Anna Kournikova promoted investment firms, while Martina Navratilova promoted a popular utility vehicle automobile in 2002.

Journalist Karen Stabiner described the moneymaking opportunities that began to emerge for women athletes during the 1980s: "Top women tennis players competed for $11 million in prize money in 1983 on a year-round, worldwide circuit, while their agents competed for endorsement dollars and planned investment strategies." She writes, "A national obsession with physical fitness had made sports the glamour industry of the eighties—and the new show business."[38] Some players receive endorsement offers even before their careers take off. In 1990, sponsors anticipated the enormous popularity of thirteen-year-old Jennifer Capriati and had signed her to contracts totaling $5 million in commercial endorsements before she had even played her first match. As teenagers just entering the pro tour, Venus Williams and her sister Serena Williams also received offers to endorse clothing and other products.

Some players who are not ranked at the top become celebrities and earn profitable contracts because of their appearance and charisma. As of 2000, nineteen-year-old Anna Kournikova had never won a major title but was famous for her pinup calendars and product endorsements. The tall, attractive blonde earned about $10 million in endorsements, and her photograph appeared so often in various newspapers and magazines, ranging from sports to fashion to news publications, that one sportswriter said she "may well be the most pho-

Tennis beauty Anna Kournikova poses in one of her many product endorsements.

HISTORIC MATCH

In perhaps their greatest match and one of the best in history, John McEnroe and Bjorn Borg met on center court at Wimbledon in July 1980. The players were known for their different styles and personalities—the cool, well-mannered Borg contrasted with the fiery, often verbal John McEnroe. Julian Rubinstein, writing at www.sportsjones.com, described them this way:

> Mac was 21, with long curly hair springing out in all directions from a red headband, a nasty, unreadable serve, and an unorthodox, tumble-foot-and-hop move to the net that would inspire a generation of serve and volleyers. . . . Borg, the stoic 24-year-old Swede, was lean and chiseled, with loping strides and smooth, classical strokes.

The match tested their stamina as well as their ability for almost four hours. Over and over, each player gained an edge, only to be frustrated by the other. The two men battled more than one hour in the fourth set alone, which McEnroe finally won in a tiebreaker: 18–16. Likewise, the fifth set went back and forth until Borg won eight games to six. When the final

Bjorn Borg falls to his knees after defeating John McEnroe in the 1980 Wimbledon finals.

tally was made, Borg had won 242 points to McEnroe's 240. Rubinstein quotes McEnroe years later, saying, "I'm just glad to have been a part of something that special. It's certainly one of the highlights of my career."

tographed woman on the face of the earth."[39] Kournikova was also ranked by Lycos as the number one downloaded athlete on the Internet. One of her representatives at Adidas sportswear said of her broad-based appeal, "Who else crosses all the boundaries—the whole spectrum, all over the world?"[40]

Turning Pro at a Younger Age

Lured by great earning potential, more tennis players begin turning pro and even winning top tournaments at increasingly younger ages. Karen Stabiner points out that young players "had the chance for independent wealth before they were old enough to vote, and celebrity status that extended far beyond the grounds of [the U.S. Open.]"[41] Tennis was also one of only a few sports where women could earn large incomes and become celebrities.

Following the boom of the 1970s, more children learned to play the game at young ages. Sometimes they began lessons as toddlers, using short-handled rackets as they took their first strokes. The most talented young players studied with top professionals and spent hours practicing each day. Many were eager to begin earning money quickly, and some even quit high school to pursue their tennis careers. In earlier decades, players had usually finished high school, and many of the top players attended and even completed college.

By the 1980s, teenage players were a fixture in top tournaments. In 1989, for example, only one of the Grand Slam singles champions was over age twenty-one. One of these "teen wonders" was American Tracy Austin. In 1977, the petite fourteen-year-old Californian became the youngest person ever to compete at the U.S. Open since 1887. By 1978, she ranked in the Top Ten female players worldwide and became the youngest woman to play on the U.S. Wightman Cup and Federation Cup teams. By age seventeen, Austin was ranked number one in the world, and the Associated Press named her Female Athlete of the Year

twice before she turned twenty. An automobile accident in 1983 derailed Austin's competitive career. Another American, Andrea Jaeger, won seven national tennis titles by age thirteen, including the girls' national sixteen-and-under clay court singles and doubles titles. In 1980, fifteen-year-old Jaeger became the youngest semifinalist ever to play in the U.S. Open, and she also reached the quarterfinals at Wimbledon.

The parents of promising young athletes often made financial sacrifices, expending a great deal of money for tennis instruction, tennis camps, equipment, and travel expenses to and from various tournaments. Young people eschewed the normal activities of adolescence, such as extracurricular activities, dating, and spending time with friends, in order to attend lessons, practice for hours each day, and compete in junior tournaments.

Many young players and their families relocated, sometimes even moving to a different country, in order to study full-time at a prestigious tennis training center. Many of these training centers are located in Florida and California, where the climate enables people to play outdoors year-round. For example, at age eleven, Monica Seles left Yugoslavia to enter Nick Bolletieri's academy in Florida. Bolletieri later wrote about Seles's tremendous drive, saying, "[She was] tireless, persistent, dogged. She worked

Monica Seles delivers a swift backhand return. Seles had earned millions in prize money and endorsements by the time she was twenty.

hard from the moment she stepped on the court. . . . She would hit the same shot over and over and over till she had it down. Not for an hour. Not for a day. For weeks."[42] Before Seles reached her teens, commercial sponsors were offering to finance her career with hundreds of thousands of dollars to be repaid with future endorsements. Her effort paid off: By age seventeen, she had won four Grand Slam titles and was ranked number one. Within three years, Seles had won $7 million and earned millions more in endorsements.

In the early 1990s, Jennifer Capriati played her first pro match at age thirteen in Boca Raton, Florida, and reached the finals before losing to Gabriela Sabatini. That spring, at age fourteen, Capriati became the youngest player ever to reach the semifinals of a Grand Slam tournament, the French Open, and she attained a ranking of number eight in the world. With an age of fifteen years, five months, eight days, she was the second youngest semifinalist at the 1991 U.S. Open, next to Jaeger. That same year, she became the youngest-ever semifinalist at Wimbledon, where she upset Martina Navratilova. While there, Capriati also became the youngest player in Wimbledon history to win a match. Sportswriters noted that when she played Seles in one final, their combined ages were only thirty-three years.

Similarly, younger men joined the pro tour, and some took center stage. At seventeen, Sweden's Mats Wilander became the youngest player ever to win the French Open, after defeating Guillermo Vilas in 1982. American Pete Sampras won the U.S. Open in 1990 just after turning nineteen.

While most players started out by playing in the junior tours, others took a different route to the top. During the 1990s, the Williams sisters, Venus and Serena, began their pro careers early and immediately joined the women's circuit. After Venus Williams turned pro in 1994 at age fourteen, she amazed onlookers by defeating a

In 1991, Jennifer Captriati became the youngest player in Wimbledon history to win a match and advance to the semifinals.

Serena Williams quickly advanced to the women's circuit after going pro in the early 1990s.

player with six years' experience. She also managed to win a set against the number two–ranked player in the world, Arantxa Sanchez Vicario. As a new century began, the trend toward younger players turning pro remained strong.

Critics Call for Changes

A number of people criticized the trend toward players turning pro in their young teens and pointed out the kinds of problems this could cause. Some critics said the pressure of competition and a grueling practice and tournament schedule could harm young players both physically and emotionally. Critics claimed that some young players appeared apathetic and isolated, unwilling to communicate much with fans or accept guidance from adults. They sometimes quarreled with officials or used profanity on the court, which can result in suspensions from the tour. Sally Jenkins, a well-known tennis sportswriter, wrote, "Teenage champions turn pro too early and often burn out or become monsters while tennis authorities fail to discipline or educate them, afraid to offend the source of all the [money]."[43]

BACK TO THE OLYMPICS

In 1984, after a sixty-four-year absence, tennis returned to the Olympics. Men's singles and doubles had been part of the games when they debuted in 1896, and women's doubles and mixed doubles matches were added in 1900. Between 1906 and 1924, women's singles were also featured. But tennis was eliminated as an Olympic sport in 1924 because of disagreements over how to run the competition and debates over amateurism, although it was included briefly as a demonstration sport in 1968, meaning that victors received honorary medals.

In 1984, the International Olympic Committee (IOC) agreed that tennis would be featured again as a demonstration sport at the Summer Games. Tennis finally returned as a full medal Olympic sport in 1988, and Steffi Graf and Czech Miloslav Mecir took home gold medals in the singles matches.

In Sydney, Australia, in 2000, Yevgeny Kafelnikov and Venus Williams won the gold medals in the singles competition. After Kafelnikov defeated Germany's Tommy Haas in five grueling sets in the final round, Gary Stocks, in his article "Kafelnikov Wins Epic Final," found at www.olympics.smh.com.au, quotes Haas as saying, "I talked to myself. . . . 'You came all the way here to play the final match in the Olympics and if you lose that match you are going to regret it for the rest of your life.' That's what kept me motivated today."

Venus Williams, who defeated Russia's Elena Dementieva in the women's final, expressed particular pleasure that she and her younger sister Serena won the gold medal in women's doubles, the third consecutive Olympics in which U.S. women took that prize. The two sisters, ages twenty and nineteen, defeated the Dutch team of Kristie Boogert and Miriam Oremans 6–1, 6–1. According to sportswriter Linda Pearce, in "Williams Sisters Add Gold Medal to Family Album," found at www.olympics.smh.com.au, Venus commented, "For me it's almost bigger than the singles, it's right up there. A victory like this with my sister, my best friend, doesn't happen often. It's very rare."

Steffi Graf in mid-serve at the 1992 Olympic Games in Barcelona, Spain.

Sportswriters actively joined the debate, claiming that an emphasis on prize money was fueling this trend and hurting the game. In 1994, Jenkins wrote,

> Tennis is spoiled rotten. If you are wondering exactly when a wonderful game became such a lousy sport, the answer is, the first time a corporate executive gave a 14-year-old a stretch limo to play with. To the average sports fan, tennis is played by pampered, insolent children, run by over-tanned businessmen and governed by quarrelsome organizations.[44]

In response to this controversy, tennis associations debated whether to set age limits on tournaments or implement other new rules that would limit the number of events a young teenage player could enter. The WTA addressed these concerns in 1994 by changing certain rules. The association limited the number of WTA events in which women under age eighteen could compete each year. As of 2002, tennis governing bodies, sportswriters, and the players themselves were still debating these issues.

CHAPTER 5

Kings and Queens of the Court

Of the many outstanding players in history, some stand out for special achievements or "firsts." They embody champion qualities: athleticism, stroke mastery, competitiveness, footwork, and speed. At times, champions reach new heights because the competition forces them to play even better in order to win.

Given the changes in court surfaces, equipment, and playing styles, it is both difficult and unfair to compare players from different eras. Tennis writer Al Laney says, "The comparing and rating of athletes who were not contemporaries and did not encounter one another on important occasions, is a trap in which no tennis reporter of experience should be caught."[45] Nobody knows who would triumph if yesterday's best players, using the same equipment and the new styles of play, met today's stars. Here are some outstanding players, both past and present.

Suzanne Lenglen

Talented, stylish, emotional—Suzanne Lenglen makes every list of the all-time greats. Born in 1899, she grew up in Nice, France, where her father, a secretary at the tennis club, taught her the game. By age twelve, Lenglen excelled, and by fifteen, she was igniting crowds.

When the French and world championships resumed in 1920 after World War I, Lenglen, now twenty years old, had command of her game. Spectators were entranced by her grace and compared her to a ballerina. Lenglen relied mostly on ball placement and speed. Fellow player Duncan Macaulay wrote:

> Suzanne never slogged the ball hard, but she hit it with adequate pace and absolute control. Her service was well placed and had a nasty swerve which took you right out of court. Her footwork was wonderful, and she had almost uncanny anticipation so that she was always in the right position to take the ball as she wanted to take it, from anyplace on the court.[46]

Lenglen captured the French title and Wimbledon in 1920, then won three major events in 1921—the French, World, and Wimbledon. She was ranked number one in 1925–1926, the first year rankings were compiled. When she turned professional in 1926, her achievements included six Wimbledon singles and six French Championships. That year, wearing high-fashion tennis dresses, she endorsed perfumes, tennis rackets, and sportswear as she played matches in the United States. At age thirty-nine, Lenglen died of anemia. She was inducted into the Hall of Fame in 1978.

Top-ranked Suzanne Lenglen at Wimbledon, in 1926.

William "Bill" Tilden

William T. "Bill" Tilden II was America's first tennis celebrity. Born in 1893 in Philadelphia, Tilden showed little ability when he started playing tennis in his teens, but he spent hours perfecting his game. At age twenty, Tilden won the U.S. mixed doubles championship at Forest Hills with his partner Mary K. Browne—a feat they repeated again in 1914. That year, Tilden was ranked number six among American men, but for several years, he played inconsistently.

After losing in the finals of the 1919 U.S. Championships, he began hitting hundreds of balls each day to polish every

Bill Tilden with a sweeping deep-court backhand at the 1929 Wimbledon finals.

stroke. As Tilden began to dominate his competitors with brilliant tennis, he also drew fans with his theatrical flair. Clad in immaculate whites, the six-foot-three, confident Tilden sometimes deliberately lost a set so he could stage a dramatic comeback. He relied on long rallies with diverse shots, rather than decisive serves or volleys.

In 1920, Tilden became the first American man to win Wimbledon and, from 1920 to 1926, he won the U.S. Men's Championship. When he turned professional at age thirty-eight, Tilden had three Wimbledon singles titles and seven U.S. singles titles, as well as the National Clay Court, National Indoor, and National Hard Court crowns. During World War II, Tilden played in exhibition matches for U.S. Army troops.

In 1969, a group of sportswriters named Bill Tilden the best tennis player of all time. His book *Match Play and the Spin of the Ball* is considered a classic. In it, he wrote, "There is no sensation in the sporting world so thoroughly enjoyable to me as that when I meet a tennis ball just right in the very middle of my racquet and smack it, just right, where my opponent should be but is not."[47]

Helen Wills

Known as "Little Miss Poker Face" for her intense concentration, Helen Wills won numerous titles during the 1920s and

Helen Wills maintains her poise during the 1924 Olympic Games.

1930s. A London sportswriter once commented, "She crushed opposition like a machine."[48]

While growing up in Berkeley, California, Wills played tennis for long hours, and she continued to practice diligently during high school. At age sixteen, Wills reached the finals of the U.S. National Championships. Spectators were surprised that this slim girl in pigtails could hit so hard, but Wills explained she modeled her forehand after William Johnston's. Her serve was also swifter and more forceful than most other women's. She usually stayed near the baseline, pounding out ground strokes until her opponent erred.

While majoring in art at college, Wills won gold medals at the 1924 Olympics for women's singles and doubles. She dominated tennis for years, winning eight Wimbledon singles titles, seven U.S. singles championships, four French singles championships, and sixteen Wightman Cup victories. From 1927 to 1932, Wills won every set she played. Back problems sidelined her in 1934, but she returned in 1937 as Mrs. Helen Wills Moody to win her last Wimbledon singles title at age thirty-two.

Rod Laver

Speed, great strokes, and concentration were the hallmarks of "the Rocket," who won two Grand Slams, more than any other individual player. For ten years, Laver led men's tennis with his mighty left arm and ability to come back from behind. Born in 1938 in Australia, Laver won the first of his three Australian singles titles in 1960. Just two years later, he won the Grand Slam, the first man to achieve that feat since Don Budge won all four majors in 1938, then set a new record by winning another Grand Slam in 1969.

1962 Wimbledon champion Rod Laver crouches for the return.

Laver wielded huge topspin on both sides. As author Eugene Scott notes, "Before Laver, the vicious topspin forehand had been used only as an experiment or a bizarre change of pace. The fleet Aussie developed it into a potent weapon. . . . Laver similarly revolutionized the backhand . . . by imparting so much spin to his backhand that the ball dipped at the net rusher's feet."[49]

In 1971, he dazzled spectators at the Tennis Champions Classic by winning thirteen straight matches. His earnings that year totaled $292,717, a record for tennis players at that time, and Laver also became the first player to earn more than $1 million. At age thirty-seven, he was still ranked in the world's Top Ten. During his career, Laver captured twenty major singles titles, including two French, two U.S., four Wimbledon, and three Australian.

Margaret Smith Court

Born in 1942, Margaret Smith Court revolutionized women's tennis by lifting weights and playing against top men to develop her game. With broad shoulders and a muscular five-foot-eleven physique, she won more major titles than any other woman before Billie Jean King, who said, "I call her the Arm because of her amazing reach."[50] She is also one of only a few players to win a Grand Slam (1970).

Between 1960 and 1975, Court won a staggering sixty-two titles in singles, dou-

Australian Margaret Smith Court teeters on an injured ankle in a milestone victory over Billie Jean King at Wimbledon in 1970.

bles, and mixed doubles. They included ten Australian singles titles, five French, three Wimbledons, and seven U.S. In the memorable 1970 Wimbledon singles final, Court played against King with a painful sprained ankle. They went to forty-six games, the longest number ever played there, before Court finally won. Known for her modesty, Court retired to have three children after her marriage in 1967, then returned to play tennis until 1977. She was inducted into the Hall of Fame in 1979.

Billie Jean King

Tennis historians have called Billie Jean King the person who has done the most to advance women athletes and the game itself.

Growing up in California, Billie Jean Moffett was a natural athlete who told her mother she would someday "be the best at something."[51] After finding out that women could not play major league baseball, she took up tennis. Later she recalled, "As good as I was, and as much as I loved tennis right from the start, I found myself out of place there, too, because it was a country-club game then, and I came from a working-class family. My father was a fireman, and we didn't have any money for rackets, much less for proper tennis dresses."[52]

King practiced diligently, especially her serve and volley, and by age sixteen, she ranked number nineteen in the United States. She rose to number four the next year and won the Wimbledon ladies' doubles title with her partner, Karen Hantze—the youngest pair ever to win that title.

After entering college as a history major, she met Larry King, who was studying law, and they were married in 1965. Meanwhile, in 1963, she reached the Wimbledon finals but lost to Margaret Smith (Court). King left college to practice tennis year-round. In 1967, she achieved a major goal by winning the Wimbledon women's singles title (as well as the doubles and mixed doubles,

Despite chronic knee injuries, Billie Jean King continued to play tennis professionally.

called a "triple") and the U.S. Championships. She won Wimbledon again in 1968 and 1969, as well as the Australian Open. At age twenty-nine, she managed to defeat teenage Chris Evert at Wimbledon in 1973.

King's many "firsts" include: first woman to sign a contract to play pro tennis; first woman athlete to earn one hundred thousand dollars in a year; first (and only, as of 2001) person to win twenty Wimbledon titles, breaking a record set in 1914; first president of the Women's Tennis Association (WTA), which she helped to found; and first woman to coach male players (for World Team Tennis).

During her thirties, King was still playing, although chronic knee injuries were holding her back. Besides writing about tennis, she has appeared as a television commentator and coached the U.S. women's team for the 2000 Olympics.

Jimmy Connors

Fast and fiery, with natural talent and an explosive two-handed backhand, James Scott Connors never gave up in a match. From 1974 to 1978, Connors was ranked the number one male player in the world.

At age three, Connors began playing tennis in 1955, taught by his mother Gloria, a tennis professional. They moved from Illinois to California when he was a teenager so he could work with Pancho Gonzales and Pancho Segura. As a student at UCLA, the left-hander won the NCAA

Jimmy Connors delivers a smashing backhand at Wimbledon in 1980.

and outstanding return of serve on both sides.

Although Connors did not dominate men's tennis after 1978, he continued winning tournaments. During his twenties, Connors sometimes clashed with officials over line calls and other matters, but later he became what Bud Collins called "a respected elder."[53] Fans were excited when he won the U.S. Open and Wimbledon in 1982 and another U.S. title in 1983. Connors also drew admiring cheers in 1989 when he upset Stefan Edberg in the fourth round of the U.S. Open to reach the quarterfinals at age thirty-seven. He was still competing in his forties.

When he retired, Connors had won 109 tournaments and earned $8,641,040, placing him fifteenth on the prize list. His charisma and dynamic style had boosted the game. Sportswriter Mike Lupica says, "Connors was the tennis boom in [the United States]. . . . Connors put tennis on TV."[54]

men's singles title in 1971, then left college in 1972 to turn pro.

His second year on the tour, Connors won the U.S. pro championship. He did even better in 1974, capturing the Australian, U.S. Open, and Wimbledon titles. Because he played in the World Team Tennis league, he was banned from competing in the French Open, which meant he could not try for a Grand Slam that year. Connors won four more U.S. Open singles titles (1976, 1978, 1982, and 1983) as well as a second Wimbledon (1982). He was known for his great speed

Chris Evert

During the 1970s, Christine Marie "Chris" Evert became one of the world's top players and inspired others to learn the game. Nicknamed "the Ice Maiden" because of her calm, disciplined manner, she relied on consistent, accurate forehand and backhand ground strokes, hit deep into her opponent's side, and on accurate shots that passed them when they moved toward the net.

The second of five children, Evert was born in Fort Lauderdale, Florida, where her father was a manager and tennis pro at a public tennis park. When she began playing at age six, she showed natural ability. She had trouble holding the racket firmly with one hand during the backhand stroke, so her father taught her to use both hands—later she popularized this "two-handed backhand" shot.

By her teens, Evert was winning junior tournaments and playing adult women. She impressed the tennis world in 1969 by defeating the great Margaret Court. While maintaining a B average in high school, Evert joined the pro circuit at age sixteen. When she arrived at the 1970 U.S. Open,

PLAYER AND COACH: JOHN McENROE

Fiery, brilliant, controversial—John Patrick McEnroe turned pro in 1978 after winning the National Intercollegiate singles as a freshman at Stanford University. At age eighteen, in 1977, he won his first major title at the French Open. The left-hander next impressed fans at Wimbledon, where he reached the semifinals before losing in four sets to Jimmy Connors. McEnroe won the U.S. Open in 1979, 1980, 1981, and 1984 and took three Wimbledon singles titles, in 1981, 1983, and 1984. Before he retired in 1992, he was ranked the number one male player in the world for four years in a row and achieved a singles match record of 849–184. Competitive zeal, speed, and a superb volley were major factors in his success.

During his competitive career, McEnroe was also known for his temper. He sometimes faced fines and suspensions for using abusive language in speaking to court officials.

Although some top players had not taken part in Davis Cup competition, McEnroe supported the team, which he first joined in 1978, saying that he felt it was important to play for his country. He set a record for the number of years

Lefty John McEnroe makes a miracle scoop at the Wimbledon finals.

played (twelve) as well as the number of singles victories (forty-one). He also played doubles and won fourteen of fifteen Cup doubles he played with partner Peter Fleming. McEnroe went on to coach the U.S. Davis Cup team.

Chris Evert braces for her widely popularized "two-handed backhand."

she had won forty-six consecutive singles events. She reached the finals but lost to Billie Jean King, who praised Evert as a great player who brought positive attention to tennis.

At seventeen, Evert reached the Wimbledon semifinals but lost to Evonne Goolagong. However, Evert triumphed when they met

two months later in the finals of the U.S. Clay Court Championships. The next year, she turned professional and began earning numerous victories, including seven French Opens (1974, 1975, 1979, 1980, 1983, 1985, 1986); six U.S. Opens (1975–1978, 1980, 1982); and three Wimbledons (1974, 1976, 1981). In 1974, she also won the Canadian and Italian titles, accumulating thirty-five titles by June. From 1973 to 1986, Evert won at least one Grand Slam title annually. *Sports Illustrated* magazine named her the 1976 "Athlete of the Year," the first woman to receive that honor, previously called "Sportsman of the Year."

Evert was one of the youngest ever to play Wightman Cup tennis. During her years on the team, 1971–1985, the United States won eleven times and Evert won all twenty-six of her singles matches. She also became the first female player to earn $1 million, a figure that reached about $9 million during her twenty-year career.

Evert continued to play during the 1980s and reached the finals of the Virginia Slims tournament in Boca Raton, Florida, where Steffi Graf defeated her in three sets. In 1989, she played Federation Cup tennis, winning all five of her singles matches. She retired that year with 157 singles titles—more than any female player in history—including 18 Grand Slam titles.

Bjorn Borg

By age twenty-one, Sweden's Bjorn Borg had already won the Italian men's title, the U.S. Pro Championships, and the French, as well as bringing Sweden to its first Davis Cup victory (1975). When he retired at the young age of twenty-six, he had maintained his streak of thirty-three Davis Cup singles victories, a record as of 2002.

Bjorn Borg straddles the baseline.

Born in 1956, Borg began playing tennis with a racket his father won in a Ping-Pong tournament and perfected a baseline game, hitting patiently until his opponent missed. The cool-mannered Swede was known for his stamina and somewhat jerky strokes. Bud Collins writes, "A player of great strength and endurance, he has a distinctive and unorthodox style and appearance. He is bowlegged, yet very fast. His muscular shoulders and well-developed torso give him the strength to lash at the ball with heavy topspin on both forehand and backhand."[55]

Although his forte was slow courts, Borg strengthened his serve and volley, which enabled him to win on the fast grass courts of Wimbledon in 1976. He defeated Jimmy Connors in 1977 and 1978 to take three straight Wimbledons. Borg tied a record set in 1913 by winning four in a row in 1979, then snagged a fifth in 1980. He also set a men's record at the French championships by winning six times. In his short pro career, Borg earned $3,609,896 in prizes.

Martina Navratilova

Martina Navratilova broke records during the 1970s and 1980s with her powerful serve and volley game. Born in Revnice, Czechoslovakia, in 1956 to an athletic family, Navratilova began playing tennis at age six. By age eight, she reached the semifinals of a twelve-and-under tournament; two years later, she won the national fourteen-and-under championships. The muscular left-hander aspired to play like her idol, Rod Laver. She later wrote, "The kids knew I loved tennis and they'd ask, 'Martina, what are you doing with all the tennis?' and I'd think to myself, Ah, one day you'll know."[56]

After winning the Czech national indoor title in 1972, Navratilova headed for the United States winter pro circuit, including the 1973 Virginia Slims and United States Tennis Association (USTA) tours. By 1975, she was reaching the final rounds of every major tournament she en-

tered and decided not to return home. Czechoslovakia was then part of the Soviet bloc, and it restricted travel and other activities of its people. That fall, Navratilova asked the U.S. government for asylum and eventually became a citizen.

During the next two years, Navratilova gained weight and seemed to lose her concentration. She resolved to improve her fitness and control her emotions on court. In 1978, she won seven consecutive Virginia Slims events. That June at Wimbledon, she

Martina Navratilova raises the Wimbledon Trophy after her victory over Chris Evert in the 1978 Wimbledon women's finals.

and Chris Evert played an exciting finals match where they split the first two sets. In the final set, Evert won four games in a row, but Navratilova fought back to win that set 7–5 and achieve the first of her record-breaking nine Wimbledon singles titles.

Between 1982 and 1987, Navratilova was ranked number one in the world for all but twenty-two weeks. In 1983, she achieved the doubles "Grand Slam" by taking the U.S. Open, Australian Open, French Open, and Wimbledon titles during the 1983–1984 season. She won her 158th pro title in 1992. When Navratilova retired from singles events in 1994, she had earned over $19 million, more than any other female player and most men. She continued to play and won both the doubles and mixed doubles titles at Wimbledon in 1995.

Ivan Lendl

Born in Czechoslovakia in 1960, Ivan Lendl was number one in the world four years (1985–1987 and 1989) and particularly dominated the U.S. Open, where he reached eight men's singles finals. Sportswriters called him the consummate professional: hardworking and fit, with good speed and anticipation.

Both Lendl's parents were tennis champions, and he grew up playing the game. As a member of the Czech Davis Cup team, he helped them win their first championship (1980). Then, between 1980 and 1983, the right-hander, known

YOUNGEST MAN TO WIN WIMBLEDON

Born in 1967 in Lieman, West Germany, Boris Becker grew up playing both soccer and tennis but began focusing on tennis at age twelve. In 1983, 1984, and 1985, he was the German junior men's champion. At age seventeen years, seven months, in 1985, Becker became the youngest man to win Wimbledon—or any other major championship, although Michael Chang set a new record in 1989 when he won the French Open at seventeen years three months.

The red-haired right-hander proceeded to win two more Wimbledon titles (1986 and 1989) as well as the U.S. Open (1989), two Australian Opens (1991 and 1996), and a record-setting forty-nine ATP singles titles. During those years, he faced stiff competition, especially from Stefan Edberg, Mats Wilander, and Ivan Lendl. In 1991, Becker was ranked number one in the world for the first time, and he was ranked in the Top Ten eight times during his nine years as a pro. He earned more than $5 million during his competitive career.

Becker was a demonstrative player whose talent and style appealed to spectators. As Bud Collins writes in his *Modern Encyclopedia of Tennis:* "A big man (6-foot-4, 180) playing a big, carefree game of booming serves, heavy forehand, penetrating volleys, and diving saves, he was an immediate crowd favorite."

Ivan Lendl in 1986, two years after becoming a U.S. citizen.

for a powerful baseline game featuring strokes with topspin, won 36 of the 101 tournaments he entered. In 1982, Lendl achieved the third-longest winning streak of the open era—forty-four consecutive matches.

As of 1992, Lendl led all previous male players in prize money, with $19,172,627. That year, after having lived in the United States since 1984, Lendl became a U.S. citizen. Despite his outstanding record, he never won Wimbledon, although he reached the finals twice and the semifinals three times.

Pete Sampras

Sportswriter Darryl Richards sums up the impact of the man who was ranked number one for several years during the 1990s by calling Pete Sampras "an unparalleled combination of power, grace, efficiency, and dignity."[57] He has also been praised for being neat, polite, and gracious to officials and fans.

Sampras was born in 1971 in Washington, D.C., one of four children in a Greek-American family. He began playing tennis seriously after the family moved to California in 1978, and by age twelve, Sampras decided to become a pro. In 1987 he made the Boys Junior Davis Cup team. Along with a strong serve-and-volley game that best suited fast courts, Sampras polished an excellent all-around game.

In 1990, nineteen-year-old Pete Sampras awed fans by winning the U.S. Open. Between 1993 and 2000, he won at least one Grand Slam title every year, including a record-breaking seven men's Wimbledon singles titles. Sampras surpassed Roy Emerson's record (twelve Grand Slam titles) when he won Wimbledon in 2000. He also won two Australian Opens (1994 and 1997) and four U.S. Opens (1990, 1993, 1995, 1996). As of 2001, he had earned more than $42 million. Noting his rocket serve and

Pete Sampras scrambles for the ball in 2002.

versatility, some sportswriters have called "Pistol Pete" the best player ever.

Steffi Graf

When nineteen-year-old Steffi Graf won Olympic gold in 1988, she was near the end of a historic year. Graf had won the Grand Slam, and her Olympic medal made it a Golden Grand Slam. A native of Bruhl, Germany, Stephanie Maria "Steffi" Graf reigned as the world's best female player during the late 1980s and early 1990s. She was known for her deadly forehand and serve, as well as enthusiasm and a down-to-earth manner.

Graf was only four years old when her father, a tennis pro, began teaching her the game. By age twelve, in 1971, she was ranked as Germany's twelfth best female player, and she turned professional the next year. Graf reached the semifinals of the 1985 U.S. Open, where she lost to Martina Navratilova. Graf rose to number four in 1986 when she reached the finals of a Lipton tournament in Florida. Chris Evert, who defeated her 6–4, 6–2, praised Graf's forehand and slice backhand. Just months later, Graf beat Evert to win her first major tournament, the Family Circle Magazine Cup.

Graf still had not won a set against arch-rival Martina Navratilova when they reached the finals of the German Open. Graf won 6–2, 6–3 before an enthusiastic home crowd. Later that year, Navratilova prevailed in the semifinals of the U.S. Open in a thrilling three-set match that featured two tiebreaker sets.

Steffi Graf celebrates after winning the 1988 French Open, sealing her second Grand Slam victory.

By 1987, Graf was on top of her game after working on her serve and backhand. She captured her first Grand Slam title—the French Open. Also in 1987, Graf won the Italian Open and Virginia Slims tournament in New York, defeating Gabriela Sabatini. With eleven wins and a record of 75–2, she earned more than $1 million that year.

As 1988 began, Graf defeated Evert at the Australian Open, then captured her second Grand Slam title for 1988 at the French Open. That year, tennis returned to the Summer Olympics as a medal sport, and Graf won in Seoul, Korea. She then defeated Navratilova at the 1988 Wimbledon with scores of 5–7, 6–2, 6–1. It had been fifty-seven years since a German had won the women's singles crown. Graf also set a new record by winning seventy-two of the seventy-five matches she played in 1988, with forty-six consecutive wins between May and November, including a U.S. Open victory over Gabriela Sabatini. Afterward, tournament officials raised the flags of the four Grand Slam countries to honor Graf's historic achievement—a Grand Slam and Olympic medal in the same year.

In 1989, Graf won another Australian Open and Wimbledon. Observers praised her speed and endurance, noting that she could run eight hundred meters in two minutes, five seconds, similar to a good college racer. Her Wimbledon victory was especially satisfying because Boris Becker was men's champion—the first time since 1934 that both winners came from the same European country. In 1989 Graf also defended her U.S. title and took another Virginia Slims title, then won the 1990 Australian. From 1987 to 1997, she never ranked below number two in the world. Graf retired in 1999.

Venus Williams

Born in Compton, California, in 1980, Venus Ebonistarr Williams showed athletic talent at a young age. Her father—and first coach—called her a "ghetto Cinderella" who would awe the tennis world. Williams strove to excel and espe-

Venus Williams waves to the crowd after winning the Nasdaq-100 Open in 2002.

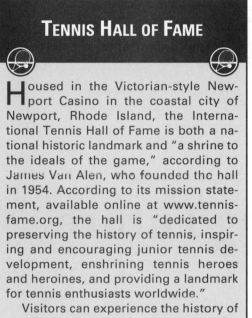

TENNIS HALL OF FAME

Housed in the Victorian-style Newport Casino in the coastal city of Newport, Rhode Island, the International Tennis Hall of Fame is both a national historic landmark and "a shrine to the ideals of the game," according to James Van Alen, who founded the hall in 1954. According to its mission statement, available online at www.tennisfame.org, the hall is "dedicated to preserving the history of tennis, inspiring and encouraging junior tennis development, enshrining tennis heroes and heroines, and providing a landmark for tennis enthusiasts worldwide."

Visitors can experience the history of tennis through interactive exhibits, videos, and memorabilia. The enshrinee hall honors great players, coaches, administrators, and tennis writers who have been inducted into the hall through the years.

cially admired the power games of Pete Sampras and Monica Seles.

By age ten, Williams was ranked number one among southern California players age twelve and under. The next year, her family moved to Florida where she and her gifted sister Serena studied at Rick Macci's International Tennis Academy. At age fourteen, Venus Williams became one of the youngest tennis players ever to turn pro. During her teens, she reached her full height of 6 feet 1½ inches and developed a muscular physique.

Williams surprised many by entering the women's pro circuit at age sixteen after skipping the junior circuit. At her first event, she won the first round and displayed a masterful serve, volley, and backhand drop shot. She went on to play several tournaments in 1995. Between 1996 and 2001, Williams earned twenty-one titles, including four Grand Slams, as Williams won both Wimbledon and the U.S. Open in 2000. In 2000, she also won the Olympic gold medal for singles and doubles, with her sister Serena. She successfully defended both her U.S. Open and Wimbledon titles in 2001. Fans waited to see what new records this young, talented player might set in the sport.

An Exciting Future

By the early twenty-first century, the basic strokes—forehand, backhand, serve, lob, overhead smash, and volley—remained part of tennis, but the game had become increasingly more challenging. Nearly all players work on a strong net game, which requires speed, excellent reflexes, and precision. During the 1990s and into the new century, the percentage of short points has been higher than in the past. Serves have been clocked at more than one hundred miles per hour.

Today's champions face stiffer competition and also benefit from more intensive and sophisticated training and coaching, as well as better equipment. They start training early and participate in more matches, sometimes playing two or more big tournaments per month.

Most players still covet Grand Slam titles, and winning the four-tournament "Grand Slam" remains a coveted achievement. Each "Slam" tournament tests players differently: The Australian Championships take place on rubberized hard court, and the U.S. Open is held on hard DecoTurf. Wimbledon retains its traditional grass court, while the French Open remains the only Grand Slam on clay. At the U.S. Open, men play up to five sets, while women still play up to three, settled by tiebreakers when players reach six games apiece. At the Australian, French, and Wimbledon championships, sets are played out until someone wins by two games.

Despite talented players and more media coverage, interest in tennis waned during the 1990s. Television ratings and ticket sales dropped from their highs in previous years. In 1994, 22 million Americans were playing tennis, as compared with 35 million in 1978, and racket sales declined by 22.6 percent between 1993 and 1994.

Analysts said one problem was the lack of strong rivalries. Pete Sampras dominated men's competition and won Wimbledon five consecutive years. Although Sampras had many worthy opponents, no one player consistently faced him in tournament finals. Likewise, Steffi Graf dominated women's events for several years.

In addition, top players were accused of being "boring" rather than exciting to watch. Although people had sometimes complained about foul language, racket throwing, and other emotional displays, some spectators seemed to find quieter, well-behaved players less entertaining.

Another complaint was that the ranking system confused fans. The ATP revamped it in 2000 to award points based on Grand Slams, nine top events, and the player's five best results in second-tier tournaments.

Players claimed the season was too long and included so many events it became exhausting. As a result, players skipped certain events, even Grand Slam tournaments like the Australian or French Opens. In

American Andre Agassi serves to Pete Sampras at Wimbledon in 1999. Agassi attempted and failed to achieve a victory over the long-standing champion.

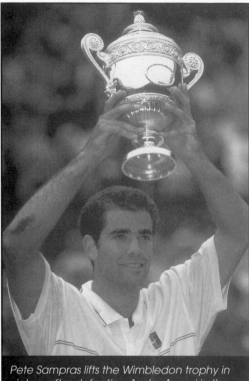

Pete Sampras lifts the Wimbledon trophy in victory after defeating Andre Agassi in the men's finals at Wimbledon in 1999.

On the upside, people noted that the game was more international and was the second most watched sport in Europe after soccer. Europeans don't have distinct sports seasons for baseball, football, basketball, and hockey, so they tend to watch tennis year-round.

Interest also rose in 2000 as the women's tour became more exciting and new players began winning. Match attendance and television audiences increased between 1998 and 2000 as Venus and Serena Williams captured top titles with their powerful games. The Sanex WTA tour matches were broadcast to hundreds of millions of television viewers around the world and attracted more than 4 million spectators to buy tickets. Steve Simmons of the *Toronto Sun* writes, "Women's tennis isn't any one player anymore. It's bigger than that, bigger than it has ever been."[59] Describing women's tennis, sportswriter Rick Reilly wrote, "The women play amazing, long, topsy-turvy, edge-of-your-seat points."[60]

In 2001, tennis audiences saw a new Wimbledon champion on center court when Croatia's Goran Ivanesevic, ranked 125th in the world, fought his way into the finals, where he was the surprise winner over Australia's Patrick Rafter. Once again, tennis had shown itself to be exciting, unpredictable, and memorable.

response, the ATP contracted with top players to play in every Grand Slam event, as well as the ATP "Super Nine" tournaments to guarantee top quality in these events. Several top players, including Pete Sampras, never competed in the Olympics because they were focusing on Grand Slam events and other tournaments. Player Boris Becker remarked, "All the withdrawals make it clear that the ATP [roster of tournaments] has to slim down. Fewer tournaments means more quality."[58]

Awards and Statistics

Wimbledon

Countries whose representatives have won the 115 Gentlemen's Singles Championships
USA (33), British Isles (32), Australia (20), France (7), Sweden (7), Germany (4), New Zealand (4), Great Britain (3), Czechoslovakia (1), Egypt (1), Netherlands (1), Spain (1), Croatia (1)

Countries whose representatives have won the 108 Ladies' Singles Championships
USA (47), British Isles (29), Germany (8), Great Britain (7), France (6), Australia (5), Brazil (3), Czech Republic (1), Spain (1), Switzerland (1)

Winners of most Gentlemen's Singles Championships

7	P. Sampras (USA)	1993–1995, 1997–2000
7	W.C. Renshaw (BRI)	1881–1886, 1889

Winners of most Gentlemen's Doubles Championships

8	H.L. Doherty (BRI)	1897–1901, 1903–1905
8	R.F. Doherty (BRI)	1897–1901, 1903–1905

Winners of most Ladies' Singles Championships

9	M. Navratilova (USA)	1978, 1979, 1982–1987, 1990
8	H.N. Wills/F.S. Moody (USA)	1927–1930, 1932, 1933, 1935, 1938

Winners of most Ladies' Doubles Championships

12	E.M. Ryan (USA)	1914, 1919–1923, 1925–1927, 1930, 1933, 1934

Winners of most Mixed Doubles Championships—Gentlemen

4	O.K. Davidson (AUS)	1967, 1971, 1973, 1974
4	K.N. Fletcher (AUS)	1963, 1965, 1966, 1968
4	E.V. Seixas (USA)	1953–1956

Winner of most Mixed Doubles Championships—Ladies

7	E.M. Ryan (USA)	1919, 1921, 1923, 1927, 1928, 1930, 1932

Winner of most Singles, Doubles, and Mixed Doubles Championships—Gentlemen

13	H.L. Doherty (BRI)	5 singles, 8 doubles 1897–1906

Winner of most Singles, Doubles, and Mixed Doubles Championships—Ladies

20	B.J. Moffit/ L.W. King (USA)	6 singles, 10 doubles, 4 mixed 1961–1979
19	E.M. Ryan (USA)	12 doubles, 7 mixed 1914–1934
19	M. Navratilova (TCH/USA)	9 singles, 7 doubles, 3 mixed 1976–1995

Winners of Singles, Doubles, and Mixed Doubles Championships in One Year—Gentlemen

J.D. Budge (USA)	1937, 1938
R.L. Riggs (USA)	1939
F.A. Sedgeman (AUS)	1952

Winners of Singles, Doubles, and Mixed Doubles Championships in One Year—Ladies

S.R.F. Lenglen (FRA)	1920, 1922, 1925
A. Marble (USA)	1939
A.L. Brough (USA)	1948, 1950
D.J. Hart (USA)	1951
L.W. King (USA)	1967, 1973

Youngest Champions

Gentlemen's Singles	B.F. Becker (GER)	17 years, 227 days (1985)
Gentlemen's Doubles	R.D. Ralston (USA)	17 years, 341 days (1932)
Ladies' Singles	C. Dod (BRI)	15 years, 285 days (1887)
Ladies' Doubles	M. Hingis (SUI)	15 years, 282 days (1996)
Mixed Doubles	R.G. Laver (AUS)	20 years, 328 days (1959)
	S.J. Williams (USA)	16 years, 282 days (1998)

Oldest Champions

Gentlemen's Singles	A.W. Gore (BRI)	41 years, 182 days (1909)
Gentlemen's Doubles	G.P. Mulloy (USA)	43 years, 226 days (1957)
Ladies' Singles	A. Sterry (BRI)	37 years, 282 days (1908)
Ladies' Doubles	E.M. Ryan (USA)	42 years, 152 days (1934)
Mixed Doubles	S.E. Stewart (USA)	42 years, 28 days (1988)
	W. duPont (USA)	44 years, 125 days (1962)

The Youngest Seeds

Gentlemen's Singles	B.R. Borg (SWE)	17 years, 19 days (1973)
Ladies' Singles	J.M. Capriati (USA)	14 years, 89 days (1990)

The Oldest Seeds

Gentlemen's Singles	R.A. Gonzalez (USA)	41 years, 45 days (1969)
Ladies' Singles	L.W. King (USA)	39 years, 210 days (1983)

Shortest Players

Gentlemen	F.H. Ampon (PHI)	1948–1953	4 feet, 11 inches
Ladies	C.G. Hoahing (BRI)	1937–1938	4 feet, 9½ inches

Tallest Players

Gentlemen	M. Srejber (TCH)	1986–1990	6 feet, 8 inches
	D. Norman (BEL)	1995	6 feet, 8 inches
Ladies	L.A. Davenport (USA)	1993–2000	6 feet 2 inches

Most Matches Played at the Championships

Gentlemen   J.R. Borotra (FRA)   223   1922–1939, 1948–1964
(Singles W 55, L 10; Doubles W 59, L 31; Doubles W 40, L 28)

Ladies   M. Navratilova (TCH/USA)   284   1973–2000
(Singles W 119, L 13; Doubles W 83, L 15; Mixed W 44, L 10)

AUS=Australia	AUT=Austria	BRI=Great Britain
EGY=Egypt	GER=Germany	SUI=Switzerland

French Championships
Winners from 1891 to 2000

Year	Men	Women
1891	H. Briggs	
1892	J. Schopfer	
1893	L. Riboulet	
1894	André Vacherot	
1895	André Vacherot	
1896	André Vacherot	
1897	Paul Ayme	Adine Masson
1898	Paul Ayme	Adine Masson
1899	Paul Ayme	Adine Masson
1900	Paul Ayme	Y. Prevost
1901	André Vacherot	P. Girod
1902	M. Vacherot	Adine Masson
1903	Max Decugis	Adine Masson
1904	Max Decugis	Kate Gillou-Fenwick
1905	Maurice Germot	Kate Gillou-Fenwick
1906	Maurice Germot	Kate Gillou-Fenwick
1907	Max Decugis	Comtesse de Kermel
1908	Max Decugis	Kate Gillou-Fenwick
1909	Max Decugis	Jeanne Matthey
1910	Maurice Germot	Jeanne Matthey
1911	André Gobert	Jeanne Matthey
1912	Max Decugis	Jeanne Matthey
1913	Max Decugis	Marguerite Broquedis
1914	Max Decugis	Marguerite Broquedis
1920	André Gobert	Suzanne Lenglen
1921	Jean Samazeuilh	Suzanne Lenglen

Year	Men	Women
1922	Henri Cochet	Suzanne Lenglen
1923	François Blanchy	Suzanne Lenglen
1924	Jean Bototra	Diddie Vlasto
1925	René Lacoste	Suzanne Lenglen
1926	Henri Cochet	Suzanne Lenglen
1927	René Lacoste	Kornelia Bouman
1928	Henri Cochet	Helen Wills
1929	René Lacoste	Helen Wills
1930	Henri Cochet	Helen Wills-Moody
1931	Jean Borotra	Cilly Aussem
1932	Henri Cochet	Helen Wills-Moody
1933	John Crawford	Margaret Scriven
1934	Gottfried von Cramm	Margaret Scriven
1935	Fred Perry	Hilde Sperling
1936	Gottfried von Cramm	Hilde Sperling
1937	Henner Henkel	Hilde Sperling
1938	Donald Budge	Simone Mathieu
1939	William McNeill	Simone Mathieu
1946	Marcel Bernard	Margaret Osborne
1947	Jozsef Asboth	Patricia Todd
1948	Frank Parker	Nelly Landry
1949	Frank Parker	M. Osborne-dupont
1950	Budge Patty	Doris Hart
1951	Jaroslav Drobny	Shirley Fry
1952	Jaroslav Drobny	Doris Hart
1953	Ken Rosewall	Maureen Connolly
1954	Tony Trabert	Maureen Connolly
1955	Tony Trabert	Angela Mortimer
1956	Lewis Hoad	Althea Gibson
1957	Sven Davidson	Shirley Bloomer
1958	Mervyn Rose	Zsuzsi Kormoczy
1959	Nicola Pietrangeli	Christine Truman
1960	Nicola Pietrangeli	Darlene Hard
1961	Manuel Santana	Ann Haydon
1962	Rod Laver	Margaret Smith
1963	Roy Emerson	Lesley Turner
1964	Manuel Santana	Margaret Smith
1965	Fred Stolle	Lesley Turner
1966	Tony Roche	Ann Haydon-Jones
1967	Roy Emerson	Françoise Durr
1968	Ken Rosewall	Nancy Richey
1969	Rod Laver	Margaret Smith-Court
1970	Jan Kodes	Margaret Smith-Court

Year	Men	Women
1971	Jan Kodes	Evonne Goolagong
1972	Andres Gimeno	Billie-Jean King
1973	Ilie Nastase	Margaret Smith-Court
1974	Bjorn Borg	Chris Evert
1976	Adriano Panatta	Sue Barker
1977	Guillermo Vilas	Mima Jausovec
1978	Bjorn Borg	Virginia Ruzici
1979	Bjorn Borg	Chris Evert-Lloyd
1980	Bjorn Borg	Chris Evert-Lloyd
1981	Bjorn Borg	Hana Mandlikova
1982	Mats Wilander	Martina Navratilova
1983	Yannick Noah	Chris Evert-Lloyd
1984	Ivan Lendl	Martina Navratilova
1985	Mats Wilander	Chris Evert-Lloyd
1986	Ivan Lendl	Chris Evert-Lloyd
1987	Ivan Lendl	Steffi Graf
1988	Mats Wilander	Steffi Graf
1989	Michael Chang	Arantxa Sanchez
1990	Andrea Gomez	Monica Seles
1991	Jim Courier	Monica Seles
1992	Jim Courier	Monica Seles
1993	Sergi Bruguera	Steffi Graf
1994	Sergi Bruguera	Arantxa Sanchez
1995	Thomas Muster	Steffi Graf
1996	Yevgueny Kafelnikov	Steffi Graf
1997	Gustavo Kuerten	Iva Majoli
1998	Carlos Moya	Arantxa Sanchez-Vicario
1999	Andre Agassi	Steffi Graf
2000	Gustavo Kuerten	Mary Pierce

Australian Championships

Most successive singles

Men:	Roy Emerson	(5)	1963–1967
Women:	Margaret Smith	(7)	1960–1966

Most successive doubles

Men:	Adrian Quist	(10)	1935–1950
Women:	Martina Navratilova /		
	Pam Shriver	(7)	1983–1989

Triples (singles, doubles, mixed doubles)

Men:	John Hawkes	1926
	Jean Borotra	1928
	Jack Crawford	1932

Women:	Daphne Akhurst	1925 / 1928 / 1929
	Nancye Wynne Bolton	1940 / 1947 / 1948
	Thelma Long	1952
	Margaret Smith	1963

Most Number of Titles (includes one shared title)

Men

Player	Years	Singles	Doubles	Mixed	Total
Adrian Quist	1936–1950	3	10	0	13
Jack Crawford	1929–1935	4	4	8	11
John Bromwich	1938–1950	2	3	1	11
Roy Emerson	1961–1969	6	8	0	9
John Newcombe	1965–1976	2	5	1	8

Women

Player	Years	Singles	Doubles	Mixed	Total
Margaret Court	1960–1973	11	8	3	21
Nancye Wynne Bolton	1926–1951	6	10	4	20
Thelma Long	1936–1958	2	12	4	18
Daphne Akhurst	1924–1930	5	4	4	13
Evonne Cawley	1971–1983	4	5	0	9
Martina Navratilova	1975–1989	3	8	0	11

Winning Countries

The singles titles have been won by the following nationalities:

Country	Men	Women
Australia	51	43
USA	15	17
Sweden	6	0
New Zealand	2	0
Argentina	2	0
Czech Republic (incl. Czechoslovakia)	3	2
France	1	1
Germany	2	4
Yugoslavia	0	3
South Africa	2	0
Switzerland	0	3
Russia	1	0

Notes

Introduction: Tennis, Anyone?

1. Quoted in Bud Collins and Zander Hollander, eds., *Bud Collins' Modern Encyclopedia of Tennis.* Detroit, MI: Gale Research, 1994, p. xii.
2. Quoted in Eugene Scott, *Tennis: Game of Motion.* New York: Crown, 1973, p. 23.
3. Quoted in Scott, *Tennis,* p. 95.

Chapter 1: From "Game of the Palm" to Lawn Tennis

4. Quoted in Heiner Gillmeister, *Tennis, A Cultural History.* London: Leicester University Press, 1997, p. 174.
5. Quoted in Scott, *Tennis,* p. 32.
6. Quoted in E.C. Potter Jr., *Kings of the Court: The Story of Lawn Tennis.* New York: A.S. Barnes, 1963, p. 1.
7. Quoted in Al Laney, *Covering the Court: A Fifty-Year Love Affair with the Game of Tennis.* New York: Simon and Schuster, 1968, p. 249.
8. Quoted in Potter, *Kings of the Court,* p. 286.
9. Quoted in Potter, *Kings of the Court,* p. 26.
10. Quoted in Collins and Hollander, *Modern Encyclopedia of Tennis,* p. 420.
11. Lou Eastwood Anderson, *Tennis for Women, with Special Reference to the Training of Teachers.* New York: A.S. Barnes, 1926, p. 47.

Chapter 2: Country Clubs to Public Courts

12. Quoted in Caryl Phillips, *The Right Set.* New York: Random House, 1999, p. 287.
13. Quoted in Potter, *Kings of the Court,* p. 245.
14. Laney, *Covering the Court,* p. 248.
15. A. Wallis Myers, "The First Davis Cup Matches," in Allison Danzig and Peter Schwed, eds., *The Fireside Book of Tennis.* New York: Simon and Schuster, 1972, p. 502.
16. Laney, *Covering the Court,* p. 189.
17. Quoted in Jeane Hoffman, "The Sutton Sisters," in Danzig and Schwed, *Fireside Book of Tennis,* p. 74.
18. Laney, *Covering the Court,* p. 211.
19. Fred Perry, "Little Bit of Luck," in

Phillips, *The Right Set,* p. 84.

20. Scott, *Tennis,* p. 71.

21. Mary Hardwick, "Maria Bueno Is Women's Champion Again," in Danzig and Schwed, *Fireside Book of Tennis,* p. 829.

22. Quoted in George Sullivan, *Queens of the Court.* New York: Dodd, Mead, 1974, p. 67.

23. Pancho Gonzales, "The Lowdown on Amateur Tennis," in Phillips, *The Right Set,* p. 96.

Chapter 3: A Booming Professional Era

24. Quoted in Potter, *Kings of the Court,* p. 302.

25. Harry Gordon, "Roy Emerson," in Danzig and Schwed, *Fireside Book of Tennis,* p. 405.

26. Gonzales, "Amateur Tennis," in Phillips, *The Right Set,* p. 93.

27. Potter, *Kings of the Court,* p. 322.

28. Laney, *Covering the Court,* p. 264.

29. Quoted in Fred Tupper, "Federation Votes for Open Tournaments," in Danzig and Schwed, *Fireside Book of Tennis,* p. 852.

30. Collins and Hollander, *Modern Encyclopedia of Tennis,* pp. 163–64.

31. Linda Timms, "Bournemouth: The World's First Open," in Danzig and Schwed, *Fireside Book of Tennis,* p. 850.

32. Lance Tingay, "The Peaceful Revolution," in Danzig and Schwed, *Fireside Book of Tennis,* p. 857.

33. Quoted in Collins and Hollander, *Modern Encyclopedia of Tennis,* p. 320.

34. Sally Jenkins, "In the Age of Compact Discs, Pete Sampras Is a Vinyl LP," *Sports Illustrated,* February 9, 1995, p. 18.

35. Title IX.

36. Collins and Hollander, *Modern Encyclopedia of Tennis,* p. 197.

37. Quoted in Collins, and Hollander, *Modern Encyclopedia of Tennis,* p. 197.

Chapter 4: A Popular Commercial Sport

38. Karen Stabiner, *Courting Fame: The Perilous Road to Women's Tennis Stardom.* New York: Harper and Row, 1986, p. 11.

39. Frank Deford, "She Won't Win the French Open, But Who Cares?" *Sports Illustrated,* June 5, 2000, p. 94.

40. Quoted in Deford, "She Won't Win," p. 94.

41. Stabiner, *Courting Fame,* p. 11.

42. Nick Bolletieri, "Grooming Monica," in Phillips, *The Right Set,* p. 107.

43. Sally Jenkins, "Tennis Is Spoiled Rotten," *Sports Illustrated,* May 9, 1994, p. 78.

44. Jenkins, "Spoiled Rotten," p. 78.

Chapter 5: Kings and Queens of the Court

45. Laney, *Covering the Court,* p. 206.

46. Duncan Macaulay, "Lenglen at Wim-

bledon," in Danzig and Schwed, *Fireside Book of Tennis,* p. 136.

47. William Tilden, *Match Play and the Spin of the Ball.* New York: Arno Press, 1925, p. xi.

48. Quoted in Robert T. Condon, *Great Women Athletes of the Twentieth Century.* Jefferson, NC: McFarland, 1991, p. 111.

49. Scott, *Tennis,* p. 80.

50. Quoted in Collins and Hollander, *Modern Encyclopedia of Tennis,* p. 343.

51. Billie Jean King with Frank Deford, *Billie Jean.* New York: Viking Press, 1982, p. 11.

52. King with Deford, *Billie Jean,* p. 13.

53. Collins and Hollander, *Modern Encyclopedia of Tennis,* pp. 340–41.

54. Mike Lupica, "The Player (Jimmy Connors)," *Tennis Magazine,* September 1992, p. 163.

55. Collins and Hollander, *Modern Encyclopedia of Tennis,* p. 336.

56. Martina Navratilova with George Vecsey, *Martina.* New York: Knopf, 1985, p. 11.

57. Darryl Richards, "Even Sampras' Historic Run Hasn't Gotten American Fans into the Game," *Dallas Morning News,* January 17, 1999, p. 21B.

Epilogue: An Exciting Future

58. Quoted in Richards, "Sampras' Historic Run," p. 21B.

59. Steve Simmons, "The Last Word," *Toronto Sun,* August 18, 1999, p. 110.

60. Rick Reilly, "Disadvantage, Women," *Sports Illustrated,* July 16, 2001, p. 92.

For Further Reading

Virginia Aronson, *Venus and Serena Williams*. Broomall, PA: Chelsea House Publishers, 2000. Biography written for young people about the dynamic Williams sisters who are electrifying the world of tennis at the turn of the twenty-first century.

Tracy Austin, *Beyond Center Court*. New York: William Morrow, 1992. Austin describes her quick rise to the top ranking spot in 1980, followed by back injuries in 1983 and a 1989 car accident that cut her career short.

Tom Biracree, *Althea Gibson*. New York: Chelsea House, 1991. Biography of the pioneering African-American player who won top honors in tennis, then became the first black professional woman golfer.

Richard Condon, *Great Women Athletes of the Twentieth Century*. Jefferson, NC: McFarland, 1991. Profiles of tennis players include Althea Gibson, Billie Jean King, and Chris Evert.

Trent Frayne, *Famous Tennis Players*. New York: Dodd, Mead, 1977. Includes profiles of great players of the 1950s, 1960s, and 1970s. Written for young people.

———, *Famous Women Tennis Players*. New York: Dodd, Mead, 1972. Profiles Althea Gibson, Billie Jean King, Margaret Smith Court, and Chris Evert. Written for young people.

Bill Gutman, *Modern Women Superstars*. New York: Dodd, Mead, 1978. Top women tennis players are included in these profiles of great athletes from the 1960s and early 1970s. Written for young people.

R.R. Knudsen, *Martina Navratilova, Tennis Power*. New York: Viking, 1986. Young adult biography of the nine-time Wimbledon champion and one of the best ever to play the game.

Victoria Sherrow, *Pete Sampras*. Berkeley Heights, NJ: Enslow Publishers, 1996. Biography of the five-time Wimbledon winner and great champion some people call the greatest ever to play the game.

George Sullivan, *Queens of the Court*. New York: Dodd, Mead, 1974. Profiles Chris Evert, Billie Jean King, Althea Gibson, and other great women players.

Works Consulted

Books

Lou Eastwood Anderson, *Tennis for Women, with Special Reference to the Training of Teachers*. New York: A.S. Barnes, 1926. This early instruction book for tennis teachers focuses on training female players.

Arthur Ashe, *A Hard Road to Glory: A History of the African-American Athlete Since 1946*. New York: Warner Books, 1988. Ashe describes the black athletes who broke new ground in various sports, including tennis.

Arthur Ashe and Arnold Rampersad. *Days of Grace*. New York: Knopf, 1993. An inspiring memoir by the world's first African-American international male tennis champion, known for his social activism and courage as well as his game.

Associated Sports Staff, *The Sports Immortals*. Englewood Cliffs, NJ: Prentice-Hall, 1972. Includes profile of Bill Tilden and other champions.

Jeanne Cherry, *Tennis Antiques and Collectibles*. Santa Monica, CA: Amaryllis Press, 1995. This heavily illustrated book contains beautiful color photos of tennis equipment, clothing, and other memorabilia, along with information about the history of these items.

Bud Collins, *My Life with the Pros*. New York: Dutton, 1989. A memoir that follows the career of Bud Collins.

Bud Collins and Zander Hollander, eds., *Bud Collins' Modern Encyclopedia of Tennis*. Detroit, MI: Gale Research, 1994. A comprehensive view of the sport, its history, players, equipment, and tournaments by the well-known sportswriter and commentator Bud Collins.

Allison Danzig and Peter Schwed, eds., *The Fireside Book of Tennis*. New York: Simon and Schuster, 1972. Absorbing collection of articles by players and sportswriters gives a first-hand look at the game—its creation, tournaments, rivalries, and controversies—from its roots in Britain into the beginning of the open era.

Althea Gibson with Richard Curtis, *So Much to Live For*. New York: Putnam, 1968. This autobiography describes the life of a great champion and first African-American player to enter major tournaments and win Wimbledon and U.S. Open.

Heiner Gillmeister, *Tennis: A Cultural History*. London, England: Leicester University Press, 1998. Gillmeister offers a comprehensive and fascinating look at the evolution of tennis from its beginnings in medieval France to the Davis Cup matches of the early 1900s.

Pancho Gonzales and Dick Hawk, *Tennis: The Complete Tennis Book*. New York: Avenel Books, 1962. This how-to book by Gonzales, one of the all-time great players and coaches, includes a biography of the author.

Will Grimsley, *101 Greatest Athletes of the Century*. New York: Crown, 1987. Top tennis players such as William Tilden are included in these profiles of outstanding twentieth-century athletes.

Laura Hilgers, *Steffi Graf*. New York: Time Magazine, 1990. Biography of the outstanding woman player who won the "Golden Grand Slam" in 1990 and demonstrated her all-court game on every kind of surface, with a topspin forehand some consider the best ever.

Helen Hull Jacobs, *Beyond the Game*. London: J.B. Lippincott, 1936. Jacobs, a tennis player and author of tennis fiction for young people, describes her career on and off the court.

Billie Jean King with Frank Deford, *Billie Jean*. New York: Viking Press, 1982. King describes her life, beginning with a sports-loving childhood in Long Beach, California, and her successful career as a tennis player and advocate for women's sports.

Al Laney, *Covering the Court: A Fifty-Year Love Affair with the Game of Tennis*. New York: Simon and Schuster, 1968. This memoir, written by one of the first journalists to specialize in tennis reporting, gives an eyewitness look at the tennis greats and the most important matches from the 1920s through the 1960s.

Grace Lichtenstein, *A Long Way, Baby: Behind the Scenes in Women's Pro Tennis*. New York: Morrow, 1974. Inside look at how women's tennis expanded in the 1970s with lucrative new tours and more recognition for players.

Frank Litsky, *Superstars*. Secaucus, NJ: Derbibooks, 1975. Includes profiles of tennis players Bill Tilden, Helen Wills Moody, and others.

Michael Mewshaw, *Ladies of the Court*. New York: Crown, 1993. Journalist Mewshaw traveled on the women's tour to get a colorful inside look at the lives of female tennis stars, such as Navratilova, Evert, Seles, and Capriati, as well as young new players.

Robert Minton, *Forest Hills: An Illustrated History*. New York: Lippincott, 1975. Detailed look at the U.S. Championships, which became the U.S. Open in 1968, including the players and great matches that took place while the tournament was held in Flushing Meadow, Queens.

Martina Navratilova with George Vecsey, *Martina*. New York: Knopf, 1985. This fascinating autobiography describes the childhood and career of the Czech-American champion whom some observers call the greatest woman tennis player ever.

E.C. Potter Jr., *Kings of the Court: The Story of Lawn Tennis*. New York: A.S. Barnes, 1963. This book covers the history of the game and its greatest players and matches from 1874 to 1962. It contains fascinating information about attempts to develop open tournaments and the debate over amateurism and professional tennis.

Eugene Scott, *Tennis: Game of Motion*. New York: Crown, 1973. This lavishly illustrated book gives a brief history and profiles of top players, important tournaments, and great matches dating from the early days of the sport to the early 1970s.

William Tilden, *Match Play and the Spin of the Ball*. New York: Arno Press, 1925. This book profiles tennis play from the first quarter of the twentieth century.

Periodicals

"Agassi Advances at ATP, and Sampras Stays Alive," *New York Times*, November 18, 1994.

Harvey Araton, "Williams Sidesteps No One," *New York Times*, September 6, 1997.

Rudolph Chelminski, "Jeu de Paume, Anyone?" *Smithsonian*, January 2000.

Christopher Clarey, "United States Surges to the Lead in Sweden," *New York Times*, September 24, 1994.

Frank Deford, "She Won't Win the French Open, But Who Cares?" *Sports Illustrated*, June 5, 2000.

Donna Doherty, "Martina Remembers Her Nine Wins," *Tennis*, July 1994.

Robin Finn, "Arthur Ashe, Tennis Star, Is Dead at 49," *New York Times*, February 8, 1993.

———, "No Doubt About It: Heat Is Up for Sampras and Sanchez Vicario," *New York Times*, January 16, 1995.

———, "Sampras, of Course, Martinez, Really?" *New York Times*, July 5, 1994.

———, "Williams Powers into Final, Where Hingis Waits," *New York Times*, September 6, 1997.

"First Black Wimbledon Champ, Althea Gibson, Recognized in England," *Jet*, July 23, 1984.

Janet Graham, "King Struck Historic Blow for Equality Twenty-five Years Ago," *Cincinnati Post*, July 23, 1998. Available on the Internet at http://www.cincypost.com.

David Higdon, "It's Sampras in Straight Sets," *New York Times,* January 30, 1994.

———, "U.S. Friends Across Net in Final Across World," *New York Times,* January 29, 1994.

Mary Huzinek et al., "Man of Grace and Glory [Arthur Ashe]," *People*, February 22, 1993.

Sally Jenkins, "In the Age of Compact Discs, Pete Sampras is a Vinyl LP," *Sports Illustrated*, February 9, 1995.

———, "I've Led a Charmed Life [Chris

Evert]," *Sports Illustrated,* May 25, 1992.

———, "Tennis: One for the Books—Steffi Graf and Yevgeny Kafelnikov, Each Made History in Winning the French Open," *Sports Illustrated,* June 17, 1996.

———, "In 1973, After Years of Trying, Arthur Ashe Wrangled an Invitation," *Sports Illustrated,* December 21, 1992.

Curry Kirkpatrick, "There She Is, Ms. America (King)," *Sports Illustrated,* October 1, 1973.

Mike Lupica, "The Player (Jimmy Connors)," *Tennis Magazine,* September 1992.

———, "The World Is Cheering Seles . . . for Now," *Sporting News,* September 11, 1995.

Kenny Moore, "Sportsman of the Year: The Eternal Example," *Sports Illustrated,* December 21, 1992.

———, "Tennis Is Spoiled Rotten," *Sports Illustrated,* July 16, 2001.

Michael J. Neill, "Pretty in White," *People,* May 10, 1993.

S.L. Price, "American Revolution: The Battle for Supremacy in the Women's Game Seemed Over After the Williams Sisters Dominated the U.S. Open as Never Before," *Sports Illustrated,* September 17, 2001.

———, "Tennis for the Ages: The Past and the Future Met in a Stirring Wimbledon Fortnight as Pete Sampras Won His Record Thirteenth Grand Slam Title and Venus Williams Her First," *Sports Illustrated,* July 17, 2000.

Rick Reilly, "Disadvantage, Women," *Sports Illustrated,* July 16, 2001.

Daryl Richards, "Even Sampras' Historic Run Hasn't Gotten American Fans Into the Game," *Dallas Morning News,* January 17, 1999.

Selena Roberts, "Williams Comes of Age, Emphatically," *New York Times,* August 30, 1997.

Steve Simmons, "The Last Word," *Toronto Sun,* August 18, 1999.

Joel Stein, "The Power Game: With Strength, Athleticism, and a Whole Lot of Attitude, Women's Tennis Has Overtaken the Sport," *Time,* September 3, 2001.

Internet Sources

Linda Pearce, "Williams Sisters Add Gold Medal to Family Album," *Sydney Games,* September 28, 2000, www.olympics.smh.com.au.

Julian Rubinstein, "Being John McEnroe," *Sports Jones,* August 24, 2001, www.sportsjones.com.

Gary Stocks, "Kafelnikov Wins Epic Final," *Sydney Jones,* September 28, 2001, www.olympics.smh.com.au.

Websites

The All-England Lawn Tennis and Croquet Club (www.wimbledon.org). The official website of the All-England Championships, better known as Wimbledon, includes history, statistics, feature articles, and information about the event, as well as a "tour" of the museum.

ATP tour (www.ATPtennis.com). The official site of the preeminent men's tour, the Association of Tennis Professionals, contains statistics, schedules, scores, news about the players, and other ATP-related news.

Australian Open (www.ausopen.org). The official website of the Australian National Championships, one of the Grand Slam tournaments, gives history, statistics, and other information about the tournament.

Davis Cup (www.daviscup.org). Describes the history, statistics, schedules, and participants for this men's international team tournament, which was launched in 1900.

Federation Cup (http://dir.yahoo.com). Offers a description of the women's international team competition that replaced the Wightman Cup: history, statistics, teams, schedule of upcoming matches, and scores.

French Open (www.frenchopen.org). The official website for this Grand Slam event, held at Roland Garros Stadium in Paris, gives history, statistics, schedules, and other information for players and fans.

International Tennis Federation (ITF) (www.itftennis.com). The ITF's official website contains a wealth of information about tennis history, rules and regulations, competitions and cups, international team events, and other material of interest to both players and fans, including links to websites for individual players.

International Tennis Hall of Fame (www.tennisfame.org). Information about this "shrine" to the history of tennis and the players who have been inducted into the hall.

Tennis.com (www.Tennis.com). This site offers information for fans and recreational players, including news about pros, tournaments, tours, and schedules, as well as articles about playing tips, fitness, and equipment, in addition to issues of *Tennis* magazine online.

TennisNet (www.TennisNet.org). This website calls itself the "premier online tennis resource," with information about tournaments, players, various tours, tennis organizations, and other materials.

U.S. Open (www.usopen.org). The official website for the U.S. National Championships includes information about the history of this event, statistics, anecdotes, upcoming tournaments, and more.

Yahoo! Sports: Tennis (http://sports.yahoo.com). This site offers numerous tennis facts, tournament results, schedules, rankings, and reprints of articles about the sport and the players.

Index

INDEX

Picture Credits

About the Author

Victoria Sherrow holds B.S. and M.S. degrees from Ohio State University. Among her writing credits are numerous stories and articles, ten books of fiction, and more than fifty books of nonfiction for children and young adults. Her recent books have explored such topics as biomedical ethics, the Great Depression, and the Holocaust. For Lucent Books, she has written *The Titanic, Life During the Gold Rush,* and *The Righteous Gentiles.* Sherrow lives in Connecticut with her husband, Peter Karoczkai, and their three children.